RUNNING *THE EDGE*

RUNNING THE EDGE

Run The Edge!

Live The Edge!

Discover the Secrets to Better Running and a Better Life

ADAM GOUCHER

TIM CATALANO

This book is available at special discounts for bulk purchases in the United
States by corporations, institutions, and other organizations. For more
information, please contact Maven Publishing www.runtheedge.com or
mavenpublishing@runtheedge.com.

Editorial production by *Marra*thon Production Services. www.marrathon.net

Designed by Brent Wilcox.

Library of Congress Control Number: 2011934093
ISBN: 978-0-61542-885-7

First Edition
10 9 8 7 6 5 4 3 2 1

This book is dedicated to all runners who refuse to settle for average or good enough; to runners who dive headfirst into their passion as they run the edge discovering their maximum potentials in both running and life. This book is for you!

CONTENTS

PART 3
Elusive Happiness

FOREWORD

Few books can teach you in a brief, inspiring read the wisdom many search a lifetime to learn.

Running the Edge is one of those rare gifts. It will take you on a journey to the center of your soul.

By committing to the lessons offered in this book, you will personally choreograph your own journey with an exciting, unrelenting quest for peak performance and discover your maximum potential both in running and in living. To quote Albert Einstein:

"Few are those who see with their own eyes and feel with their own hearts."

The wisdom offered in *Running the Edge* will place you among those few.

Billy Mills
Olympic 10k Gold Medalist

PART 1
Transformative Experiences

Without inspiration the best powers of the mind
remain dormant. There is a fuel in us which
needs to be ignited with sparks.

—Johann Gottfried Von Herder

Life can change course in a moment. Each of us has had experiences where the path we were on suddenly diverged and led us to a place we never would have imagined. Sometimes, these transformational experiences happen by chance. Other times, we consciously choose to take a different road. Some experiences alter our path only slightly, while others rock our worlds to the extent that life will never be the same.

Adam

The blood-soaked couch in the backyard and the bullet hole in our living room wall were the only physical signs remaining of the tragedy from the night before. My mom had spent hours mopping up the dried pools of blood, which had needed to remain as the police concluded their investigation. I was angry. It was easy for me to be angry in those days as an eighth-grade boy from a broken home. My normal teenage angst was compounded by my father's apparent lack of interest in my life, a house on the verge of foreclosure, and a mother who spent more time at her boyfriend's house than she did at ours.

"How are we going to afford a new couch?" This thought looped endlessly through my mind even though I knew the state of our couch and finances was not as important as the life that had been lost. I knew they were not as important as my sister Debbie, who could not stop crying, or my exhausted mother. I was fourteen, far too young to be the man of the house, powerless to help the situation. So I let my confusion turn to rage. "Somebody needs to pay for our couch!" I didn't say it out loud. Instead, I allowed the storm building inside me to soak my adolescent identity with a fury that demanded vengeance for the cruel and unfair life I was living. I hated feeling like a victim. Helpless. Powerless. Weak.

Debbie never saw the body. She had been upstairs making out with her new boyfriend when the shot rattled the house. Her friends yelled for her to stay upstairs and eventually joined her there to wait until the police arrived. She came down just as the coroner was wheeling Bobby out the front door under a sheet. She called our mom at her boyfriend's house at 2:00 A.M. to deliver the news. I was staying at a friend's house that night and overheard an early-morning phone call asking my friend's mother to keep me busy and not allow me to come home until the investigation was complete.

It seemed like days before I got a complete picture of what had happened. Debbie could not tell the story without crying, and none of it seemed to make sense. Apparently, my sister had been out with a few friends when they met up with two boys from a different school across town. The two boys were already fairly drunk and were looking for a place to keep drinking their alcohol. Debbie volunteered our house since she knew that nobody would be home. When they got to our house, the two boys continued to drink until one of them pulled out a gun. He waived it around like a toy and proposed they all play Russian roulette. Everyone else at the party told him to put it away and not to be stupid. He scoffed and told them the gun was not loaded as he put it away. The small party continued downstairs while Debbie and her boyfriend went upstairs to get some privacy.

Bobby was drunk, but he was not the boy who had brought the gun. No one really remembers how or why Bobby picked it up, but he must have believed the other boy who said it wasn't loaded. He joked about Russian roulette just before he put the barrel to his head and pulled the trigger.

I have heard many versions of this story, but they all end the same: a senseless death and my already dysfunctional family thrown further into chaos. The couch in our backyard was a silent witness to what had really happened and seemed to symbolize where my life was headed.

Before that night, I had already experimented with alcohol. Some of my junior high school friends had tried smoking marijuana and were actively trying to get their hands on more drugs. I was doing what kids like me do. I was from a poor family, with an absent father and no plans for the future. No one in my family had ever gone to college, and I had no reason to believe I would be any different. I was not interested in school, but I was a fairly good athlete, which was helping keep me somewhat in line. But the storm inside threatened to steer me even further off course. I never gave a thought to my own mortality or the idea that I could choose to be more than my circumstances were dictating. Even the accidental suicide in my house the night before was not enough to get me on a positive track. It took one final insult, one final slap in the face, to change my life.

While the police wrapped up their final investigations, I occupied myself by skateboarding in our cul-de-sac. I'd spent hours designing and building a wooden skate ramp to practice on at home. It was one of the few constructive things I had done, and it made me proud. I took a break from skating to get a drink and emerged from our garage just in time to see the last police officer pulling away from our house. My jaw dropped as I watched him drive directly over my skate ramp with his patrol car. He then put his car in reverse and backed over it again just to be sure it was completely destroyed. I will never forget the look on his face as he glanced back at me before he drove away. He looked at me as if I were trash. Worthless. A symbol of everything wrong with American youth. I could tell he had no respect for me or my family, and I believed he crushed my ramp to send me a message that I would never amount to anything.

All the anger and rage I had ever experienced paled in comparison to what I felt inside. The violent storm broke through the levy in uncontrollable screams and wrathful tears. I knew at that moment that I could not let that cop be right. I knew I had to rise above my own mediocrity and take control of my life. In my mind, it was me against the world, and I was ready to fight.

I threw myself into school and got involved in the D.A.R.E. program. I did speaking engagements at elementary schools warning kids of the dangers of drugs and alcohol. I became a peer counselor and got involved in the student government. In my senior year, I was elected student body president. Most importantly, I discovered running.

Running allowed me to control the storm. It gave me a release for the anger and frustration living inside me. When I ran, I was able to let loose the fury until I was so exhausted I could feel calm. In the hours following a run, I could see the real me. I could see my potential to be a good person. I could relax and smile and look forward to creating a better life. The memory of the bloody couch no longer haunted me. I was free.

When Tim and I were putting this book together, we looked back at our lives in an attempt to identify the transformative experiences that helped shape who we are, how we see the world, and how we see ourselves. We spent hours reflecting on how events both tragic and triumphant had influenced our lives.

Bobby's accidental death had a profound impact on my life, but the tragedy was also a transformational experience for everyone else involved. I am not sure what came of Bobby's family, but their lives probably took an even sharper turn that evening than mine did. I know that my mom transformed in many positive ways. She changed her priorities, devoted more time to her children, and became a superb mother. Debbie began to evaluate her friendships differently as she distanced herself from those who were potential bad influences, and she began surrounding herself with people who were involved in constructive activities. As for me, because of this event, I decided I would not drink again until I was an adult, and I vowed to keep my body free of drugs for my entire life.

Beyond those conscious changes, I was also transformed on a deeper level. I wanted more from my life and expected more of myself than I did before. I could not put it into words back then, but I wanted to create and live an exceptional life. I wanted to be excellent in everything. I knew that running could help me achieve many of my dreams and provide a healthy outlet for me to control the storm. I even thought that maybe if I got good enough at running, my father might take notice and become a part of my life. I put everything I had into training and racing, sometimes running away from my fears and doubts, and other times chasing not only the life I wanted but also a better version of myself.

Years later, on a recruiting trip to the University of Colorado, I had another transformative experience. I made a friend.

Tim

Two thoughts were going through my mind as the kickoff sailed toward me. First, *make sure you catch the ball*. And second, *sprint straight up the field as fast as you can*. It was only a special-teams practice during my ninth-grade year, but I wanted to impress the coaches. I had seen a kickoff returned for a touchdown on TV over the weekend, and the returner never made a cut. He just ran in a straight line past the defenders until he found the end zone. I don't know why I thought this strategy might work for me, but I was determined to give it a try.

I caught the ball already moving forward. As soon as I knew the ball was secure, I started to sprint for all I was worth. I could already see myself waltzing into the end zone, but I didn't see the enormous defender, also wanting to impress the coaches, heading straight for me. He hit me so hard that my feet flew straight into the air as the ball flew out of my hands.

One of us impressed the coaches that day; the other one became a runner.

I finished that season as a bench-warming tailback, but the memory of that hit (and my inability to get my weight up over 120 pounds) propelled me to choose cross-country over football the following year. Little did I know, the pain and suffering I would endure as a runner would be far worse than the pain of that hit, while the joy of setting a new PR (personal record) would be far sweeter than any touchdown run.

Sometimes, it is the little things that alter our course and put us on a path we hadn't previously imagined. I don't remember the name of the

guy/bus who hit me that day, but I am thankful I didn't score a touchdown and impress the coaches. If I had, I might never have discovered
the joy running brings me or experienced what it is like to run my way
to a better life.

Seven years later, during my junior year at the University of Colorado, I
hosted a brash young recruit during his official visit. He was fresh off
winning the national title at the Foot Locker championships and was the
top high school distance runner in the country. I had never heard of him.

We took him to dinner and then to a party. He had absolutely no interest in drinking and mentioned that he did not like parties where people get drunk. I remember thinking that he would fit in well with our team
since none of the varsity ever partied during the season. I remember ad-
miring his headstrong nature and conviction in his beliefs. I didn't know
it at the time, but that night, I made a friend who would change my life.

The closest I ever came to beating Adam in a race was his freshman
year, during our varsity time trial. Teammate Clint Wells and I were cruis-
ing to the finish side by side, comfortably running in second and third
position, well behind all-American Alan Culpepper. In the final five meters, a runner came blasting past us like a missile into the chute. I remember calling him a punk (or worse) and shoving him in the back.
When we got out of the chute, I pulled him aside to remind him that it
was only a time trial with nine spots open and there was no need to kick
down teammates. He shrugged and reminded me that whatever I wanted
to call it, it was still a race and he raced to win. To this day, I don't think
we have had another disagreement, and I was never close enough to
watch him finish another race.

For some reason, Adam and I clicked. His passion and fire for running and life matched my own. On our easy runs, we would run behind
the noise of the lead pack and talk about life. Several nights a week, we
would head to the gym and lift weights together to continue our bantering. Both of us wanted to be exceptional. Both of us wanted to be more
than just runners. We wanted to be great at everything we did and knew

that if we worked as hard in all areas of our lives as we did at running, we could build amazing futures.

As our own personal philosophy developed over the years, we tested many of our beliefs. We continued the dialogue as I went on to become a psychology teacher and coach and he became a professional runner. Finally, about two years ago, we started to put our ideas down on paper. Both of us realized that as good as our lives were, we could do better. We had become complacent and satisfied with good enough. If we wanted to improve our lives and truly strive for excellence in everything, we would need another transformative experience. We didn't need another tragedy or jarring hit on the football field. We needed a plan and a system of accountability to work intentionally on the areas of our lives where we wanted to improve the most. This book is the result.

Writing this book has been a tremendously emotional experience. Both of us have had to reflect not only on the joys and highs of being distance runners, but also on our own shortcomings and failures of the past. We have spent hours in front of the six "mirrors"—specific exercises in self-evaluation described in Part 2—trying to learn the difference between who we really are and who we want to be. At times, it has been difficult to admit just how many mistakes we have made and continue to make. At other times, it has been profoundly empowering to finally understand who we are and what we can become.

As both of us discover our maximum potentials in every area of life, we begin to see the edges of what is possible. Our goal in running is to get as close to that edge as we can, chasing the horizon of possibility. In our lives, we have also started to define the edges of what is possible and to define our vision of perfection. As far away as the edges might be, we want to continue taking strides to get closer to them. We have grown tremendously since beginning this book almost two years ago, but we also realize just how far we still have to go and just how much better our lives can be if we continue to run the edge.

Neither of us believes he has all the answers. On the contrary, we have a long way to go to even approach true wisdom. What we do possess is a sincere desire and ample motivation to improve ourselves. We want to put forth an intentional and consistent effort in analyzing our lives and improving our performances as runners, family members, and friends and in our careers and education.

Being a runner is truly a gift. Runners have access to a world and a set of life lessons that can transform every aspect of their lives. We want to tap into that runner's world and harness the transformative power found in the distance run. We want to use running as a teacher, motivator, and compelling force of positive change in our lives.

THE SECRET INGREDIENT

As a runner, you are like a chef preparing the perfect meal. To make yourself into the best runner you can be, you need a good recipe and all the right ingredients. Many running books can help you improve your performance through various training philosophies and systems, strength and flexibility exercises, proper diet and nutrition, and even some good reads on how to stay motivated, healthy, and focused. These books are valuable. They address many of the necessary ingredients for a complete and well-rounded runner. Our book adds another ingredient to the recipe—an ingredient that can take your running to the next level. Without this ingredient, all the training, flexibility, strength, and diet advice in the world will have little effect. This ingredient is the catalyst that makes all the other ingredients more effective.

We can learn a lot by looking at what great runners do. How do they train? What do they eat? What exercises and cross-training do they find valuable? But what we often fail to consider is what great runners are like. What personal attributes allow them to be great? Attributes such as self-discipline, tenacity, adaptability, initiative, courage, and integrity separate great runners from good ones. The presence of these often intangible attributes is the secret ingredient. It is the catalyst necessary to maximize the benefits of all the other ingredients, and it is the focus of this book.

Imagine what developing more optimism, determination, focus, and accountability could do for your running. By becoming aware of your own personal set of attributes and by reflecting on how those attributes affect not only your running, but also the other important areas of your life, you are given the insight necessary to strengthen and develop what you are like as a runner and as a human being.

C H A P T E R   1

The Gauntlet

Runners love a challenge. Their sport requires an internal drive foreign to most "normal" people. They not only push through pain, but welcome it. They live to test their limits, and if a gauntlet is thrown down, they embrace the chance to test their mettle.

THE SUMMER OF CHALLENGES

Tim

I should have been fired at numerous points during my years coaching high school distance runners. As a young coach, I lacked the judgment and wisdom supplied by maturity and experience. In the name of fun and team building, I allowed and encouraged my runners to do things a more responsible coach would have forbidden or at least discouraged. The following story is not the only one in this book where I look back and wonder what I was thinking to allow athletes entrusted to my care to do such things. I am lucky that no runners were seriously injured during some of our adventures and thankful that every one of them survived to be included in these stories.

The summer of challenges was a terrible idea. At its best, it was a painful and disgusting experience. At its worst, it was dangerous. Years later, when I was asked why so many teenage kids would choose to do such a thing, I shrugged my shoulders and replied, "They were runners."

The challenges began when Steve Curtis, an extremely skinny and overconfident high school runner, claimed he could eat twenty doughnuts in an hour. Steve was an excellent runner, but he was even better at running his mouth. When he made this bold claim, his teammates quickly threw down the gauntlet. Steve did not back down. With a sideways grin and the same faraway look in his eyes he always got when toeing the line, Steve accepted the challenge.

Two days later, after a morning run, the team gathered on the deck behind my house to witness the attempt. Steve was joined by his teammate Nick Tussing, who also believed he himself could eat twenty doughnuts and did not want Steve to have all the glory. As their coach, I should have known better, but I could not resist the fun of joining the fray. And while I was pretty sure I couldn't eat twenty doughnuts, I was confident that I could eat more than either Nick or Steve could. The rest of the team watched as the three of us attacked boxes filled with sixty doughnuts. Glazed, chocolate-frosted, and jelly-filled goodness soon gave way to pain and bloating stomachs. Nick dropped out at nine and claimed he would never eat another doughnut. Steve managed to stuff down eleven before heaving the partly digested pastries over the railing on the deck to rot in the hot July sun. I managed to eat thirteen and pretended not to be in considerable pain while I suffered quietly behind a victorious smile.

Any rational person watching these events would have been mortified by the gluttony and self-induced pain. But these were not rational people. These were high school distance runners.

Inspired by the carnage of the twenty-doughnut challenge, someone had the bright idea to hold another challenge the following week. Sixteen runners decided to participate in the *gallon challenge,* where they would see who could drink a full gallon of water in one hour. Anyone who puked or peed during that hour would be automatically disqualified.

Watching athletes suffer was nothing new for me. On occasion, I even saw their recently eaten lunch splattered on the track after an intense interval session, but none of that could have prepared me for this.

Each runner arrived to the challenge deck carrying the regulation clear, plastic gallon jug full of water. The stopwatch started, and sixteen skinny runners attempted to fill their bodies with eight pounds of liquid. Cassy was the first to puke, about thirty minutes in. One moment, she was sitting quietly in a deck chair, and the next moment, she surprised herself and everyone else as she projected half a gallon of fluid, soaking her feet and the deck. The team laughed and shouted in unison, "Disqualified!" Five minutes later, Jen was leaning over the railing. Hearing the splattering sounds on the rocks below set Erik off, and the barf festival was on. One after another, the runners ran to the rail amid laughter and shouts of "Disqualified!" When the chaos subsided, only three athletes had made it through the challenge successfully, but all of them wanted to make this an annual tradition.

Although these runners might seem a bit crazy, they were far from stupid. Their cumulative GPA was well over 3.6, and two consecutive years' valedictorians participated in this challenge. The point of these stories is not to be disgusting, but to illustrate two observations about distance runners: (1) Sometimes they are a little crazy, and (2) they love a challenge.

As we explained in the introduction to Part 1, this book is about your own personal challenge. And what is the gauntlet we are throwing down for you? It is to become a distance maven. We will describe the distance maven in detail in the following chapters, but in a few words, the distance maven is someone who is

> When I am struggling and feeling sorry for myself, I repeat the mantra "How bad do you want it?" Fortunately, I always answer, "I want it bad." It is the same in life. In moving up the ladder at work or anything else, you have to have goals and then ask yourself, "How bad do you want it?"
>
> **—Chris Solinsky**

constantly chasing an ideal in pursuit of his or her own perfection. Distance mavens are running the edge: Not satisfied with an ordinary life, they have a burning desire to live a life less ordinary or even extraordinary. They use running as a teacher and metaphor for life and all of its possibilities. They wish to test their limits and discover their maximum potential not only as runners, but also as human beings.

WHAT IS LIFE?

Before we can go any further, we need to define *life*. It is not enough to refer to life as a vague concept without a specific frame of reference. Anyone can say, "I want to improve my life." But what is this person talking about? What needs improvement? When we refer to a life less ordinary or say that we can use running as a metaphor for life, what are we referring to? We will expand on these ideas in later chapters, but for now, let's talk about life.

We divide life into five stories: education, career, family, friendships, and passions. Each of us is living these five life stories at all times. We can be successful or unsuccessful in each of them. The task in becoming a distance maven is in achieving greater success in each of your five life stories.

You can find various levels of success in each of these stories. Think of the people you know. Some are great at being fathers and mothers; others excel at their jobs or in school. Many struggle with all of these. Running is no different. As a passion, or personal interest, it is held to the same standards of success as those that apply to family, friendships, career, and education.

Virtually everything you can improve in your life fits into one of these five life stories, and each story is an active process, meaning our success or failure depends on our actions and decisions. You cannot be successful at watching television, because it is a passive process, requiring no action beyond changing the channels or volume level.

In this book, we will be looking at the lessons we can learn from running (from our passions or personal-interest life story) and how those lessons can lead to greater success, fulfillment, and satisfaction not only in running, but also in our other four stories.

Becoming a distance maven will require us to partake in a personal revolution. We will have to overthrow our own mediocrity, purge our biggest flaws, refine our strengths, and rebuild ourselves to match our own highest standards. We will get closer to the edge of our potential and create the absolute best versions of ourselves. We will dedicate ourselves to excellence in everything and learn how running can be the key to unlocking not only physical fitness, but mental and emotional fitness as well.

If you choose to take up this gauntlet, we will take you with us on the journey. We will be going through the steps with you. By illuminating the way of the maven and gazing into the six mirrors, we will uncover the key attributes embodied by distance mavens and will illustrate how runners can use their sport to excavate the potential buried within themselves. Are you ready for the gauntlet? Are you ready to become a distance maven?

> Running has influenced every aspect of my life. Starting out as a kid running allows you to learn about yourself. I was painfully shy as a child, and running helped me to be less shy and relate to other people. It allowed me to broaden my horizons.
>
> It taught me how to express my competitive instinct and desire to be good at everything. It gave me self-confidence.
>
> **—Paula Radcliffe**

IN PROGRESS

As authors of this book, neither of us pretends to be perfect. Both of us have our flaws as runners and as humans. Like most people, we have made our share of mistakes, hurt more people than we should have, and, at times, behaved poorly. Nevertheless, we have two choices. We can shrug our shoulders and accept these flaws in our character, or we can resolve to become better, make fewer mistakes, hurt fewer people, and conduct our lives in a way that makes us proud. If we choose the latter, we start the process. We put ourselves in motion to becoming more. We are in progress.

Adam

In 2005, at the USA Track and Field Championships, I finished a disappointing eighth place in the 5000 meters. I believed I was ready to run much faster and had no doubt in my mind that I would place in the top three and make the world team. What's worse, my failure to make the team was not the biggest mistake I made that day.

I was extremely disappointed and frustrated after the race, when John Meyer of the *Denver Post* approached me for an interview. I had done interviews with John before and we always shared a positive rapport. When I expressed my disappointment in the results, he looked surprised and uttered, "Really?" It was an innocent question, and he was by no means trying to provoke me. But in my frustration, my mind was clouded and I felt as if he were doubting me. I felt as though he represented all the naysayers and other detractors who had been questioning my toughness, desire, and durability for the past few years. I let my post-race emotions take over, and instead of conducting myself with class and dignity, I lashed out in anger. Instead of taking responsibility for what happened, I looked for a place to lay the blame. I claimed I was faster than all the runners who had just beaten me and guaranteed that by the end of the year, I would run faster than everyone in that race. This was an attempt to cheapen what they had just accomplished and to avoid owning my own performance. I was also taking a jab at John even though he was only doing his job as a reporter.

By the time I cooled down, the damage was done. I had let my temper and frustration trample my reputation and my image of myself. I did not view myself as a bitter or angry person, but that is how I had behaved that day, and that is certainly how I appeared to others who witnessed my actions.

On that day and many others, the gap between the Adam I was and the Adam I wanted to be was vast. Ideally, in that interview I would have given credit to the other runners. Tim Broe, Ian Dobson, Ryan Hall, Jorge Torres, Jonathan Riley, Matt Tegenkamp, and Ed Moran had beaten me that day. They deserved credit and respect for performing when it mattered. Ideally, I would have taken responsibility for my own race, accepted the result, and vowed to work even harder for my next opportunity. Unfortunately, there is often a gap between the ideal and the real.

The first steps in our journey are difficult. Before we can even begin to become the best versions of ourselves, we must first go through a painful exercise of identifying and owning our own shortcomings. We have to break down the protective walls of our egos and admit that we are not as perfect as we would like to be. We must also identify our most valuable attributes that give us strength as runners and as people. Finally, we must accept the gauntlet and choose to follow the way of the maven, as works in progress, to become better runners and better human beings. These first three steps are outlined below.

THE FIRST STEPS OF THE DISTANCE MAVEN

1. Make a list or write a short paragraph of your worst qualities.

First, take a hard look at yourself with your most critical eye. Dig out the deepest, darkest aspects of yourself that you hide from others and may not even want to admit to yourself. We all have these. We all carry with us attributes and tendencies that we wish we did not possess. These attributes prevent us from becoming the best we can be. In running, maybe you have to admit that you are occasionally lazy or that you have given up when it got difficult. In your personal life, maybe you are not always kind or unselfish. Maybe you are mean-spirited or give in to peer pressure, even though you know it is wrong.

No matter what your specific shortcomings are or how painful it is to admit to them, it is important to identify them, because they are weighing you down and preventing you from rising to your potential. In the coming chapters, you will learn how to break the chains and free yourself from these limitations. You will be free to become a better runner and a better person.

2. Make a list or write a short paragraph about your best qualities.

It is equally important to recognize that despite your faults and imperfections, you do more good than bad. You have amazing qualities that attract your friends to you. You have attributes that you treasure and like to display as often as possible. Just being a runner means you possess some initiative and self-discipline. Maybe you are kind to everyone. Maybe you are a strong leader, a good daughter or son, girlfriend or boyfriend, wife or husband, and so on. Maybe you have empathy for the less fortunate and volunteer to help.

Whatever your best qualities are, be sure to spend an equal amount of time listing them. They are the pillars that give you strength, value, relevance, and the power to break the chains holding you down.

3. Accept the challenge and take up the gauntlet.

Once you have recognized and taken ownership of your imperfections and strengths, you can dedicate yourself to improving each of your five life stories. You can start the process, take action, and begin discovering not only who you are, but also the person and runner you are capable of becoming. You will be in progress right along with us.

Tim

I am in progress. I recognize that my real self and my ideal self are not the same. I have let myself down on numerous occasions where I took the easy road and made poor choices rather than doing the right thing. Instead of taking responsibility for my choices and behavior, I have blamed others. I am guilty of being petty, bull-headed, self-righteous, arrogant, lazy, and downright mean. I have failed to accept people for who they are. I have participated in petty gossip at the expense of other people. I am not perfect.

I also recognize that I have many gifts and strengths. I am a loyal friend and family member. I have reached out to people in need. I have touched the lives of others and helped make their lives better. I believe I am a positive influence in the world and in the lives of the people who know me. I have worked hard to get to where I am as an athlete, a professional, and a human being.

I accept the gauntlet. I want to become a distance maven. I choose to rise to the challenge of becoming a better man tomorrow than I am today. I understand that it is up to me to take action to change my life. I wish to follow the path of the maven and become the best possible version of myself. I am in progress.

Adam

I am in progress. I accept responsibility for the actions of my past, where I have not lived up to my expectations of myself. I have allowed my temper to damage important relationships in my life, and I have held grudges against people who I feel have abandoned me. I have embarrassed myself and my family through my actions and words. I can be stubborn to a fault, egotistical, and judgmental. I am not perfect.

I also recognize my strengths. I am a faithful and loving husband, a reliable friend, and a dedicated member of my family. I enjoy using my time and my life to support young runners in their personal journeys. I am trustworthy and honest and do not let people down. I am kind and friendly to everyone I meet, and I believe that I am a positive influence in the lives of the people who know me.

I gladly take up this gauntlet and wish to become a distance maven. I will dedicate myself with the same determination, drive, and tenacity I have in my running to the quest of becoming a better man and a role model for my son. I will follow the path of the maven and work continuously to become the man I wish to be. I am in progress.

What is done is done. There are no do-overs. We cannot take back the hurt or the damage we have caused in our own lives or the lives of others. What we can do is turn the page and move forward. We can learn from our mistakes and strive not to repeat them. This is the way of the maven. We are not perfect, but we are now in progress!

We will refer back to these first steps throughout the book. You will have a chance to update the details, as you uncover aspects of yourself and gain a deeper understanding of who you are and who you would like to become. This is your personal reflection. You do not need to show these paragraphs to anyone else, so be as honest as you possibly can. These are only the first steps in a journey as we learn to run and live the edge.

WAY of the MAVEN

Grab a Notebook

As you read this book, look for these sections to go through the exercises with us. These boxes summarize some specific exercises you can follow as you become a distance maven. Although these exercises are optional, doing them will help you get even more out of this book. You might want to get a notebook to dedicate to this journey. A written record will help you take the exercises seriously and will allow you to monitor your thoughts, actions, and progress over time.

If you do decide to keep a written record of your progress, you can start with your pledge of the distance maven, which we outlined above. But briefly, enter the following steps in your notebook:

1. List or write out some of your weaknesses and qualities that you would like to improve. Remember to be honest. No one needs to see this but you.
2. List or write out your strengths and best qualities. This is just as important as identifying your weaknesses. From these, you can draw strength and understand that despite your flaws, you are a good person.
3. Accept the challenge! Write a statement about your commitment and your vow to work hard in the following chapters to become the person you want to be and to create the life you want to live.

Congratulations! You are now a distance maven. Welcome to the journey!

CHAPTER 2

The Runner and the Maven

The power of one is above all things the power to believe in yourself; often well beyond any latent ability previously demonstrated. The mind is the athlete. The body is simply the means it uses.

—Bryce Courtenay, *The Power of One*

"Run, Forrest! Run!" The 1994 release of the movie *Forrest Gump* did amazing things for people who like to taunt runners from behind the wheel of a car. When they see a runner striding along, an irresistible urge comes over them. They feel a need to lash out at this road warrior. In our experience, it is usually men who do the taunting, and they are almost always with a buddy riding shotgun. One of them rolls down the window, leans out, and screams the cliché "Ruuuun, Forrrrrest!" The driver then mashes down the accelerator as the vehicle speeds away in a cloud of testosterone. No doubt high fives and celebration ensue inside the cab as the men congratulate each other on how clever and funny they are.

I ONLY RUN WHEN CHASED

Adam

When I first started running in high school and college, these taunts made me angry. I would flip off the drivers or shout back at them, hoping they would have the guts to stop and confront me face-to-face. Then I came to a realization that changed my perspective. These drive-by taunters are experiencing the exact opposite effect people get from watching afternoon TV shows like *Jerry Springer*. When we see people on these shows—people who often have just discovered that their mom has been a transgender stripper for the past fifteen years—we feel better about our own, less screwed-up lives. We are happy to be us and not them. But when insecure people see a runner actively pursuing a healthy lifestyle, they are threatened and feel as if their own lives and efforts don't measure up. Faced by this threat to their ego, they attempt to salvage their self-esteem by belittling the runner.

> I was cross-training on a road bike in Michigan on a country road when this guy came up in a big truck, swearing at me and telling me to get off the road. He scared the hell out of me!
>
> **—Dathan Ritzenhein**

With this new perspective, I was able to change the way I reacted to the taunters. Instead of getting angry at them or striking back, I would smile with a deep satisfaction that I was me and not them. In these moments, when the insults and jabs are meant to bring me down and make me feel bad about myself and my chosen passion, they have the opposite effect. Instead, I feel a profound sense of peace and fulfillment in knowing that I am allowing myself to experience this gift that most people will never understand. I am thankful that I discovered a sport that frees me from needing the approval of others. I am thankful that I have a body, mind, and spirit able to get me off the couch, out the door, and onto the roads to continue my personal journey. The jeers of the faceless drivers become as meaningless as the sounds of nearby traffic, a distant train, or the chirping of birds.

WHY DO YOU RUN?

Criticism of runners goes well beyond the anonymous drivers shouting out their windows. Many people openly express their disbelief that someone would deliberately choose to run. As a runner, you have probably heard it all: "I only run when I am being chased." "How can you just run?" "I hate running!" "I don't understand how someone can run for fun!" These comments make sense if you consider them from the perspective of a non-runner, but how are we to respond? How can we justify loving a sport that other athletes view as punishment? From their perspective, it seems ludicrous to spend all this time trying to get good at what other athletes are forced to do when they are bad. Not only do we engage in a sport that most athletes associate with punishment and pain, but we love it to a degree that borders on obsession. We embrace it with a passion foreign to the uninitiated. No wonder so many people think we are nuts. So how, then, can we accurately answer the question "Why do you run?" Maybe this story will help.

> Running is like life for me. It means happiness. It means bad times. It means family.
>
> **–Kara Goucher**

Tim

Valerie walked into my high school office one day during her lunch hour. A confused and mildly upset freshman, she was struggling to figure out how high school worked. Two of her friends had joined the cross-country team, and now all they talked about were splits, personal records, blisters, intervals, *fartleks*, and other running-related topics. She noticed other changes in them as well. They seemed happier, more spontaneous and optimistic. They had more energy and were less interested in fitting into a particular group or stereotype. Valerie came to me looking for answers for why her friends loved running so much, and I suspected she was interested in giving running a try but needed a little push to be persuaded to come out for the team. Never missing a chance to recruit a new runner, I launched into my well-rehearsed recruitment metaphor.

"Pretend I am a person who can only see the world in black-and-white. Now imagine you need to explain to me what the color blue looks like. How would you do it?"

Valerie thought for a moment and then began with a confident "Blue is like . . ." She paused. Her eyes rolled up as she searched the ceiling and walls of the office for a single word that could help me understand blue. I stopped her before she tried to speak again.

"That is exactly what it is like trying to explain running to a nonrunner. Being a runner is like being able to see the color blue. When two people share these common experiences, they do not need to talk about them or try to describe them in words. But without common experience, it is difficult for me, or any other runner, to help you understand why we are so passionate about this sport. If you really want answers, you need to become a runner and develop color vision."

Valerie's eyes widened. Perhaps she was a little surprised I had asked her to become a runner after meeting her only a few minutes ago. She was staring at me speechlessly, so I continued.

"Becoming a runner and sharing in this common experience is not as easy as simply lacing up your shoes one day and going for a run. It is a journey that can take some time and determination as your body adjusts to this new activity. It is a rite of passage every runner must go through to unlock the secret all runners share, but I cannot describe it in words any better than you can describe the color blue. Once the secret is unlocked, a new level and depth of understanding emerges."

I was probably talking more to myself at this point as Valerie's wordless stare remained unchanged. "So what do you say?" I asked. "Will I see you at practice tomorrow? Are you ready to become a runner and develop color vision?"

Nothing.

"If you come out for the team, you will get to spend more time with your friends."

That was the only part of the recruiting speech she needed. Valerie came to practice every day for the next four years. Although we never talked about it again, I knew she understood what it means to be a runner and why we both loved to run.

We all run for different reasons. Some of us are philosophical about it, while others just want to share a healthy activity with like-minded friends. Whatever the reasons, runners develop a shared understanding and passion that might seem counterintuitive to a nonrunner. It is as if we have climbed a mountain and discovered a secret on the other side.

Imagine for a moment that you are a new runner trying to scale the mountain and learn the runner's secret. You want to share in that common experience and see for yourself why people love to run. Unfortunately, climbing this mountain is not easy. There is a price to pay that requires an unusual amount of determination, initiative, and commitment. Getting to the other side of the mountain might look easy for people who are fit, but for those who are not, the summit can seem insurmountable.

Put yourself in the shoes of many people when they first start running. Every step hurts. Every stride is pain. Your knees hurt. Your lower back aches. During your runs, your chest feels constricted. Even something as natural as breathing causes you discomfort. None of your body's systems seem to be working together. They are in constant conflict and discord as the heart races, the breathing is strained, and muscles rebel, burn, and feel heavy. After your runs, as you count the new blisters on your feet, you feel as if you've been hit by a truck. The conventional wisdom that running is *not fun* seems truer than ever. "How can people do this for fun?" begs a painfully obvious answer: They can't! But if you continue to run and resist all common sense and logic to quit, one day, something magical happens. One day, while on a run, you notice that running does not hurt. Not only does it not hurt, but it feels natural and easy. Your legs feel powerful and strong. Your breath, heartbeat, and muscles have found a rhythm and harmony working together in perfect balance. You get a sense that this is what humans were meant to do, and you feel a connection to your primitive ancestors, as if you have discovered what you were always meant to be. On that day, you have finally reached the top of the mountain and lived for a moment in the runner's reality. On that day, you unlocked the secret to a new understanding, just as the person who has never seen in color opens her eyes to see the color blue. You have had an experience that can never be taken away. Finally, you get it. Finally, you see and comprehend what all the fuss is about.

Like an obsession, this feeling carries you now, back to the other side of the mountain, day after day, as the passion for a new sport and new way of life emerges.

This might not be the same way you discovered running, but hopefully, imagining how a new runner might go through the process helps you understand how and why so many people develop such an intense passion for a sport others find unimaginable.

Why do we run? Running is the gift we give ourselves. Like most things worth doing, running is hard, making the fruits of our labor intensely sweet and profoundly satisfying. We run because running allows us to live in a reality where we develop a sense of enthusiasm with what others might call mundane. It is a reality that reveals the world, our bodies, and our minds to us with the same sense of wonder and discovery as seen through the eyes of a child.

ONCE A RUNNER

Adam

Running is more than a sport. It is an identity. I am not somebody who just likes to run. I *am* a runner. This is the difference between a pastime and a passion. I like to play golf, but I am not a golfer. I like to cook, but

I am not a chef. I don't *just like* to run. I *am* a runner. It is a passion. It is part of who I am and is woven into the fabric of my personality, character, and psyche. People who run to lose weight, to meet a standard for the military, or for any other purpose beyond running itself are still running but more as a pastime than as a passion. Passionate runners run because they love the feeling of running in their legs and chest. They run because running flows from their pores as easily as sweat. They chase faster times, longer runs, and better workouts for intrinsic reasons that transcend any extrinsic benefit. They run because an internal force inside of them drives them to test their limits. They run because in running, they are in the moment, in flow, living a life they chose. Runners might be losing weight, lowering their blood pressure, avoiding diabetes, and getting in their recommended daily allowance of exercise, but these are happy by-products of their passion for the activity itself. There is nothing wrong with people who run as a pastime any more than with people who play golf or people who cook as pastimes. In fact, the runner, golfer, and chef appreciate the people who run, golf, and cook as pastimes because the "pastime people" have a greater understanding of what it takes to be good at a chosen passion. They get a glimpse of the life without fully living it. But people who run merely as a pastime do not share the same understanding of what it means to be a runner. Even on my worst days, when running is not fun, or when I have to force myself to get out of bed and out the door, I am still a runner. It is still me!

Running is only one of thousands of passions people might have. Avid cyclists, rock climbers, musicians, artists, poets, coin collectors, engineers, sky divers, and mathematicians might speak in similar terms about their chosen passions. As a reader of this book, you might be able to apply many of the principles found in these pages to several of your other passions. Running the edge is a metaphor for using the energy and lessons found in running to make you successful in your other life stories. The edge represents your maximum potentials and highest aspirations, whether they be in running or your education, career, family, friendships, or other passions.

Take a moment to contemplate what else you are passionate about. As you continue to read this book, keep these other passions in mind and consider how you might also take them to the edge.

The unspoken and shared understanding of what it means to be a runner can be seen in the kinship between runners. When 40,000 people line up to run the Chicago Marathon, or when 130 line up at a high school cross-country race, they can look each other in the eye with a certain respect, awareness, and comprehension that is prohibitively elusive for the nonrunner. Before, during, and after the race, the fellowship between runners is tangible and real. The brotherhood and sisterhood of the running community can be felt in the air as they inhale a collective like-mindedness. To be a runner in the midst of other runners just before the start of a race is a mystical experience that can no more be captured in words than can the color blue.

It is not just races that fuel the runner. The runner's secret is something that runners carry with them every time they work out or set aside time in their day to visit the other side of the mountain and the runner's reality. After a workout, when they are at school or work or home, they can still feel the run in their body. That tingling sensation in their chest, legs, and arms reminds them of the gift they have given themselves. Their minds are fully awake, fully active, and fully alert. They think with a clarity only available in those fleeting hours following a run. It is their secret, and after a run, nobody can take it away. They get to walk through hallways and across plazas with a spring, if not in their step, then in their spirit. They have a signature smile on their faces, knowing what they accomplished during the hours when others were still asleep or sitting on the couch watching television. They spent time getting better. They spent time giving themselves a gift that they can keep forever. They do this because it is their passion. They run because it is who they are. Once a person has been a runner, he or she will always understand that.

Some runners live in this reality for a long time. Others get there, but lack the discipline to stay in the kind of shape necessary to remain. For a while, running shapes, defines, and colors every aspect of their lives, but as they lose fitness, they lose access to the other side of the mountain. Gone are the simple joys they once experienced in the runner's world and the benefits of being in that kind of shape. They still understand what it is like. They still know the secret, but they have let themselves deteriorate to the point where even though they understand the reality and know it exists, they have gone back to living in black-and-white, where they can no longer see the color blue. Back perhaps to a colorless existence where they do not experience that same passion for running or life. They know it is there, and they know that they can get back there anytime, if they are willing to pay the price of once again getting in shape, steeling the body, retraining the heart and lungs, and fighting their own doubts, laziness, and urges to stop.

It is the exact opposite to a drug addiction. Drug habits are easy to start, but people have to check themselves into rehab clinics to stop. Running is a drug where the stopping is easy. Getting hooked is the hard part. Runners who have fallen from the grace of their own health need to enter rehab and work like the devil to get back on the running drug.

Even if they fall out of shape and are no longer able to visit the runner's world of fitness again, they keep the secret. And because they know the secret, they never become the guys in cars feeling the urge to taunt the runner. Instead, they look at runners with a nostalgic awareness of the edge the runners are chasing and respect them for it.

THE MAVEN

In the previous paragraphs, we have attempted to describe the runner. Like people who try to capture running in words, our description of what it means to be a runner fails to encapsulate the deeper essence of what running means. The maven, on the other hand, is easy to describe.

In his book *The Tipping Point*, Malcolm Gladwell describes a maven as an expert with far-reaching knowledge in a given field and wisdom pertaining to a subject. As connoisseurs of knowledge, mavens seek not only to expand their expertise but also to share it with others. Because of their vast knowledge, expertise, and desire to share what they know to help others, mavens are very influential in their social circles.

There are many types of mavens: music mavens, car mavens, computer mavens, climate mavens, and thousands more. If you want to know what is happening in the music scene, what car or computer to buy, or what is really going on with climate change, find a maven. They will know better than just about anyone else and will be happy to share what they know to help you.

> People who have an amazing sense of positivity are great to be around and train with. When you are around them, they make you want to be a better person. They just have that aura.
>
> **–Amy Yoder Begley**

The maven we are going to be discovering in this book is the *distance maven*, a new kind of maven with a special expertise. Through this journey of self-discovery, we will not only come to understand distance mavens, but will begin building and shaping ourselves into them.

When we combine the runner and the maven, it is like lighting a fuse that causes an explosion of potential. What are distance mavens experts at? The science of training? Injury prevention and recovery? Diet and nutrition? Strength and flexibility training? Perhaps, but none of those things are distance mavens' primary purpose. In the next chapter, you will meet the distance maven.

CHAPTER 3

The Distance Maven

A SEARCH FOR COURAGE

The battles that count aren't the ones for gold medals.
The struggles within yourself—the invisible, inevitable
battles inside all of us—that's where it's at.

—Jesse Owens

I n his book *Running and Being*, Dr. George Sheehan explores the notion that war provides a context to uncover a person's greatness. He quotes the poet John Berryman: "A man can live his entire life without knowing whether or not he is a coward." Sheehan speculates that in times of peace, our day-to-day, nine-to-five lives provide little opportunity for the average person to reveal the hero inside. Something is missing, and our burning need to know ourselves goes unfulfilled.

WAR, BUNGEE JUMPERS, STREAKERS, AND THIEVES

In the absence of war, the human need for self-discovery manifests in all manner of personal challenges. Some people feel compelled to strap a stretchy cord to their ankles and jump from a bridge. Others risk their lives, fortunes, and families to scale the world's tallest mountains. Why would someone choose to leap out of an airplane, jump over fifteen school buses on a motorcycle, or run with the bulls through the streets of Pamplona? Is it the thirst for adrenaline or the need to test limits, face fears, and gain personal insight?

Even acts such as dodging security guards while sprinting naked across a sports field in front of thousands of amused fans provide an element of imminent danger missing from the normal life of the average person. We could argue that the kleptomaniac, who cannot resist pocketing items from store shelves, is starving for danger and looking for a thrill. What are we to do if life does not provide us with an authentic context to discover ourselves and explore our personal greatness? Should we live our entire lives without knowing whether or not we are cowards? Or should we seek answers in activities designed to bring us face-to-face with the parts of ourselves we may never see otherwise?

The mass appeal of running might have something to do with the human need for danger, the need to face peril and understand how we will react in a fight-or-flight situation. Each race and workout is like a minibattle in a personal war of fitness and self-discovery. Running provides the context we need to look deep inside ourselves and discover personal characteristics only visible when we push our physical limits. It may not be a life-and-death situation like true war, but it feels like one when we are in that last mile or final 100-meter sprint to the finish. In those moments, runners are almost certainly closer to actual death than the skydiver, bungee jumper, or streaker will ever get in their chosen activities. How we respond in these challenging circumstances reveals *who we are*. In these circumstances, we are able to examine parts of ourselves hidden from those who do not push these limits or choose these challenges.

CLIFF JUMPING, ENLIGHTENMENT, AND RUNNING THE EDGE

Adam

I stood on top of the cliff, peering over the edge and wishing I was anywhere else. Lake Powell should have looked beautiful from this perch, but my view was colored by fear, and all I could see was the edge. My wife Kara had already jumped into the deep waters below and was now urging me on with encouraging words. "You can do it!" she yelled from the safety of the shore. She was well aware of my fear of heights and careful not to push too hard. Tim was not as understanding. "What's up, Sally?" he yelled. "Looks like you might have a case of wuss-itis!" I wanted him to shut up, but more than that, I wanted just to push off the ledge and get it over with. I made a move, bent my knees, but then froze and wobbled backward as Tim laughed and zoomed in closer with the video camera. In my head, I knew that I was being irrational and that the probability of death or even major injury was minimal from only thirty-five feet up. Still, I could not force myself to jump. The encouraging words from my wife and the sarcastic jeering of my best friend faded away as the dialogue in my own mind consumed me and became all I could hear. "Just do it," I told myself in one thought, which was followed immediately by, "It's not worth it. Just walk away." Fight or flight. Round and round I went for what seemed like an eternity before inexplicably, I felt myself lunging forward and then falling with my arms and legs spiraling for balance. I surfaced moments later with only one thought in my mind: "I *have* to do that again!"

In the moments following that jump, I felt the same euphoria I get in the moments after a good race or a hard workout. I had faced a fear. I had overcome self-doubt. I had pushed my limits and emerged unscathed.

I was now armed with the most important affirmation a person can have. The affirmation "I can!"

Although runners may seek a cliff to jump, find a mountain to climb, or decide to run with the bulls, they do not need to worry about whether they are cowards. They have daily evidence to the contrary, and even in a time of peace, they are able to fight personal battles on the roads and trails.

So if being a runner provides the context to test our courage, then being a maven provides the awareness, inquiry, and analysis of what is happening. What is revealed to distance mavens in these moments of courage is profound insight into our own nature. We are able to examine essential qualities and instinctive drives of the human race dating back hundreds of thousands of years, before social pressures suppressed our animalistic nature. We can see with unparalleled clarity who we really are.

Becoming a distance maven takes effort, reflection, and focus. These insights do not come solely from running. We have to know what to look for, and we have to spend time reflecting on what is learned from each battle. Only by being *aware* of what occurs in ourselves while we are on the edge, pushing our limits, facing our doubts and fears, can we make the changes necessary to become a distance maven. Without this awareness, we are still satisfying a human need just like the adrenaline junkie who runs with the bulls, but we don't empower ourselves to become more than what we reveal in those moments. In other words, what we discover about ourselves remains stagnant. Despite our deeper understanding, we do not attempt to develop or grow from the experience.

While the adrenaline junkies search for answers about themselves through often extreme actions, other people pursue the same answers through extreme thought. Many of the questions are the same, but the methods could not be more different. The thinkers often meditate, do yoga, go on retreats, read books, and pay psychologists huge sums of money to answer the question "Who am I?" Like the streaker, they are

Side Note to Self

The distance maven is first and foremost an expert of self. But what is the self, and how are we attached to or separate from ourselves? Maybe a little fun with the concept of the self will help us understand it better. So ask yourself, "Self, who am I?"

The point is that we talk about our "selves" all the time but rarely do we stop to consider what the self is. What we need here is a "self" concept.

The self is a difficult thing to describe, but most broadly, we can look at it as the core of our being, in which the qualities that make us who we are can be found. In other words, the self is what makes you, you. No two selves are alike. Mine and yours may be similar, but they are not the same. For now, we just need to define the self as those qualities in us that lead to our individual ways of behaving, thinking, and perceiving the world. Distance mavens use running as a way to better understand themselves. With this greater awareness comes the power to improve not only in running but in each of the five life stories.

involved in the universal human quest for meaning, enlightenment, and self-discovery. However, unlike the bungee jumper, they are not searching through action and experience but rather through thought and reflection.

The distance maven combines the best of both these worlds and gets it all for free. Combining action with thought contributes to a more complete personal insight than can be achieved using only one technique. We can find our answers on the roads, on trails, and in races as we are given mental space to reflect, learn, and grow. In pursuing our passion with a purposeful mind, we uncover secrets others spend a lifetime searching for.

In this chapter, we do not intend to paint a complete picture of distance mavens or to detail all the attributes that mavens possess. Rather, we want to provide a snapshot and background to illustrate the overall concept. In Part 2 of the book, we outline the six attributes embodied by distance mavens and how these attributes are shared not only by successful runners but also by people who excel in their other life stories. Running provides the existential experience or real action the runner needs, just as jumping out of a plane provides it for the skydiver. Follow the action of running with purposeful thought and reflection we describe in the chapters that follow, and you, too, will be running the edge, chasing the ideal you!

SELF-ACTUALIZATION AND PEAK EXPERIENCES

What would an ideal version of oneself look like? Psychologists, philosophers, and poets have been asking this question for centuries. Although there is no one-size-fits-all ideal self that will be the answer for every individual, some common themes and representations might speak to you.

The psychologist Abraham Maslow described his version of an ideal person as "self-actualized." He claimed that less than one percent of humans ever achieve self-actualization, but that we all continuously strive for it:

> What a man *can* be, he *must* be. This need we may call self-actualization . . . It refers to the desire for self-fulfillment, namely, to the tendency for him to become actually what he is potentially. This tendency might be phrased as the desire to become more and more what one is, to become everything that one is capable of becoming.

Maslow believed that people could become self-actualized artists, musicians, writers, poets, scholars, and athletes. Although he never heard of the term *distance maven*, we believe he would have agreed that runners can also become his self-actualized ideal.

For those 99 percent of us who are unable to achieve self-actualization, Maslow claimed that we can get a glimpse of what it is like to be self-actualized by having "peak experiences." He described these peak experiences as "moments of intense joy, wonder, awe and ecstasy. After these experiences, people feel inspired, strengthened, renewed or transformed." Another term for the adrenaline junkies we discussed earlier would be *peak-experience junkies*. Adam's jumping off the cliff was certainly a peak experience, and both of us have found many peak experiences in our running careers.

The goal in running is to always keep improving for as long as you can. When I moved to Portland, it became clear to me that it was also time for me to improve in areas of my life outside of running. I proposed to Julia on the day we moved out here, and I started the happiest time of my life up to this point. This experience put both life and running into perspective, and it was that prototypical moment of self-discovery for me, where I realized that even in those times when my running is not going well, life is still good.

–Alan Webb

Tim

I was in my third year as a teacher and a coach when one of the brightest freshmen in our school—a student who seemed to have the world by the tail—took his own life. On a chilly Monday morning, I walked into the school thinking it would be a week like any other, but the tear-stained faces lining the halls signaled otherwise. When I learned the news, I immediately went into counseling mode, trying to help my students process the loss, deal with their anger, and sort through their confusion. My own head and emotions were a mess, but I needed to maintain my composure and attempt to provide guidance and support.

Five days later, I finally had a chance to escape for a while and drove to Boulder to run some of my favorite trails from college. I had what Maslow would call a peak experience when suddenly the clouds in my mind lifted and I found clarity. The next morning, I sat down and wrote the following letter to my team:

The events of the last week leave me with a heavy heart and a philosophical mind. I have spent six days trying to make sense of my emotions about the death of Alex Davis [not his real name]. At first I was in shock and denial, and then I became angry at Alex for what he did. Later, I was just sad for his loss and for the pain of those who knew and loved him. Then on Saturday, as I was running alone through the snow-covered trails in the mountains of Boulder, I stopped. I looked up through the pine trees at the blue sky. Snow was melting and dripping from the branches. In the wintery silence, the only sounds were my own heartbeat, my breath, and the drops of water falling on the unmelted snow. I stood there for several moments soaking in the peaceful beauty of this spot, and I cried. I cried because I had found a perfect moment in time. Running has given me hundreds of such moments, but this time was different because I wanted to show it to Alex. I wanted to show it to everyone feeling sad. I wanted to share my joy in that moment with everyone I knew, but I was alone. Some people will never find such a moment. Others will pass them by without another thought. Runners are lucky in that they often find themselves in places where every stride is a perfect moment. The rest of my run was like that for me. I was truly happy to be alive and able to run. I loved feeling the fatigue building up in my legs and lower back as I ran on and on. The more exhausted I became, the more alive I felt. When I finally ended my scheduled 45-minute run, I had been running for 1 hour and 38 minutes. I was completely drained of energy and fluids, yet I was happier than I had been in weeks.

Every day is a gift. Each time the sun rises, a new day full of possibilities and experiences begins. Some days are more exciting than others, but I am resolved to enjoy each day for whatever it brings, and appreciate it for the gift that it is. Running is one of the best things that has ever happened to me. I hope that you can find as much happiness and peace in it as I have. I hope you find many perfect moments through running, whether it is in crossing the finish line of a race, or in the middle of an ordinary training run.

For me it is now Sunday morning 9:15. My body is feeling the effects of yesterday's run, but I can't wait to lace up my shoes and head out the door. By 10:00 I will be chasing yet another perfect moment and I will be thinking of you.

My experience that day closely matches Maslow's definition of a peak experience. It was a moment of intense joy and wonder. I did find myself inspired, strengthened, renewed, and transformed. It was the medicine I needed that day, a gift for my aching soul, an affirmation of a beautiful life.

According to Maslow, the perfect moments or peak experiences described above give us insight into the life of a self-actualized person. To be fully self-actualized was Maslow's version of the ideal self.

Maslow detailed many characteristics of self-actualized people in an attempt to describe what they might be like. According to Maslow, self-actualized people

- have realistic perceptions of themselves, others, and the world around them
- are concerned with solving problems outside of themselves, including helping others
- have a few close, intimate friends rather than many superficial relationships
- are excited and interested in everything, even ordinary things
- value independence and solitude and need time to focus on developing their own potential
- are not susceptible to social pressures, often being seen as a nonconformist
- are creative, original, and fun
- often have peak experiences
- have a sense of humor directed at themselves or the human condition, not at the expense of others

- are democratic, fair, and nondiscriminatory—embracing and enjoying all cultures, races, and individual styles
- take responsibility for choices

Some of Maslow's characteristics might speak to your ideal self, while others may not. It would be absurd to believe that every person's ideal self would be the same. Likewise, when you look at the qualities of distance mavens, some qualities will appeal to you more than others, but you can choose your own version of your ideal self and then begin to construct it as you run the edge.

THE SELF-ACTUALIZED DISTANCE MAVEN

When putting together the concept of the distance maven, we combined not only Maslow's theory of self-actualization but also Carl Rogers's "fully functioning person," Lewis Goldberg's five-dimension personality model, and the several-thousand-year-old Asian concept of the warrior poet.

As we looked through the literature at desirable attributes of an ideal person, we held two very strict criteria: first, each attribute must be one that can be learned, developed, or enhanced through running. Second, each attribute has to have the ability to improve not only a person's running, but also each of the person's five life stories (education, career, family, friendships, and passions).

We avoided making a list of negative attributes for two reasons. First, in Chapter 1, we already suggested that you list your own negative qualities in your pledge to become a distance maven. Second, as you develop these positive attributes, you will find that many of the negative qualities will fade away on their own.

The following list of positive qualities of distance mavens is, of course, not exhaustive. Readers no doubt could add other qualities that they have found to be important. Distance mavens:

- have a sincere desire to learn, grow, and become a better person
- reject the idea of living a normal or an average life, wanting to be excellent in everything, not just running
- understand that they are the hero in their life stories and that it is up to them and their actions to create the life they want to live
- use running as a tool to understand their own strengths and limitations
- believe life should be fun and challenging—that they should play as hard as they work and work as hard as they live
- have abundant knowledge and skill to live a successful and fulfilling life
- are confident, optimistic, and full of initiative, that is, are driven to take action
- have empathy for others and know how to work on a team; are friendly, honest, and kind
- are self-disciplined, reliable, accountable, and determined
- are flexible and open-minded
- are spontaneous and creative, appreciating all experiences, both good and bad, and develop deep, meaningful, and lasting relationships
- have a sense of humor and can laugh at things beyond their control
- are constantly inspired and inspiring

A lot of my biggest moments in life have been letting things go. For example, forgiving my stepfather and the strength that this gave me to move on in my life. Or in competition, when I stopped obsessing over wanting to beat specific people. My whole life had been centered around beating this person or holding this grudge; then I finally opened my eyes and saw how that was just dragging me down and holding me back from my life. A lot of my biggest moments have been when I have just let those things go. It is like the weight of the world is off my shoulders and then I can refocus on what is important.

–Kara Goucher

This might seem like a lengthy list, but each of us is a complex being with many facets. If our goal is excellence in everything, then we must work on our lives from many directions.

What makes a person a distance maven is not necessarily how many of these qualities he or she possesses, but rather the desire and consistent dedication to self-improvement by working on weaknesses and developing strengths. Running works the same way. We analyze where we are in our running today and then take the necessary steps to becoming a better runner tomorrow. This process then becomes a guide for how we can improve in each of our life stories.

As outlined in the introduction, we are all in progress. None of us is perfect, and we never will be, but we can dedicate our efforts both in running and in life to become closer and closer to our ideal. This is the definition of running the edge.

WAY of the MAVEN

A "Shopping List" for Self-Actualization

Go back to the two lists on pages 43 and 45. Identify which attributes of the self-actualized person and the distance maven you already possess. Write them down. This list represents aspects of your real self as you are right now.

Now go back to the lists and look at the attributes you would like to possess. Write these down as well, but separate them from the attributes you already possess. This part of the list represents some aspects of your ideal self. You will continue to refine and develop the difference between your real and ideal self as you go through the book. These lists are only part of the bigger picture. You will use them for direction in your own personal revolution.

CHAPTER 4

Because It's Hard

The doughnut-eating and gallon-drinking challenge stories from Chapter 1 illustrate an important side of the distance runner. The sport of running is hard. Most people cannot bring themselves to do it long enough to get to the other side of the mountain. They give up and accept that they will never understand the color blue because running is too hard. Strangely, it is precisely this aspect of running that draws so many people to the sport. Many people express the desire to run a marathon someday. They are enchanted by the idea in their most winsome moments because they know it will provide a supreme test of their strength and determination. Despite the allure, most of these people will never follow through on this desire and will look upon those who have done marathons with a sense of awe and admiration.

If running were easy, it would lose its seduction as an exclusive club reserved for the fit and tenacious. If it were easy, tens of thousands of people who pay money to register for local 10K runs or who commit huge chunks of time to train their bodies to withstand the pounding of an ultra-marathon would choose other, more challenging pursuits. Yes, running is hard, and that is exactly what makes it so irresistible to those of us lucky enough to understand.

SOMEDAY IS TODAY

Adam

It was mid-July between my sophomore and junior years of college. Summer training was going well. Tim and I had just finished a twelve-mile easy run and were slamming down slice after slice of a French toast breakfast feast. The conversation turned to the topic of "someday." Both of us hated the idea of *someday*, where people put off what they really want to do until some unknown point in time that will most likely never come. The first time we had had this conversation, I had told Tim that I had always wanted to learn to scuba dive. He exclaimed, "Me too! Wouldn't it be great to go scuba diving someday?" With these words, a recurring conversation began, and so did a lasting friendship. Both of us agreed that when possible, "someday" should be now. If there is no reason other than laziness standing between us and what we want to do, then, someday is today. Of course, this does not apply to aspirations like "I want to have kids someday," or "I would like to build my own house someday." In situations like these, there are obvious reasons to wait and keep someday at a nonspecific date in the future. But for activities like learning to scuba dive, for which there was no reason to wait, someday can and should be right now.

> I never would have thought I could replace a sink or a garbage disposal, but I have done things like that. Running has proven to me that being stubborn can be beneficial. I think to myself, "I know I can do this. I know I can figure this out, and I am going to keep trying and approach the problem from every angle until I get it figured out."
>
> **—Chris Solinsky**

We signed up for scuba classes through the recreation center at the University of Colorado (CU), and before we knew it, we were driving to Mexico over spring break to finish our certification and to do our first open-water dives. It was an epic trip (a story we may tell you "someday"), and both of us resolved to live the rest of our lives with the philosophy that if you can live your dreams today, then you should.

So on this mid-July day, after a good run and a gluttonous breakfast, the familiar conversation came up again.

"I have always wanted to ride my bike to Fort Collins," Tim said.

"But you don't have a bike," I replied.

"That does not change the fact I want to try it."

The facts were these. Neither Tim nor I rode bikes. I had an old mountain bike my mom had bought for me from Target for a hundred dollars when I was in high school. The cobwebs under the seat betrayed that it had not been moved in years, as did the lack of air in the tires. Tim didn't even own a bike after he had left his Huffy on campus three summers ago and had come back from summer break to find it stolen. Our best estimation was that neither of us had even sat on a bike in over three years!

"What are you doing today?" I asked, and Tim instantly knew where this was going. Both Tim and I had committed to purging the words "I have always wanted to" from our vocabularies whenever possible, and this adventure would be just the latest in a long line of impulsive things we did trying to live our motto.

We spent the next two hours cleaning up my bike, filling the tires, and finding a bike for Tim to borrow. His brother Scott had an old camouflage mountain bike in about the same repair as mine. Though he laughed at us when we told him what we intended to do, he quickly gave us permission to use it.

We each grabbed a water bottle and began our journey during the hottest part of the afternoon. Neither of us had any idea how long the fifty-mile ride between Tim's house in Boulder and his parents' house in Fort Collins would take, but we hoped to arrive in time for a free home-cooked dinner.

By the time we reached Longmont fifteen miles into the trip, we were both complaining about sore butts and lamenting our lack of foresight to use sunscreen. Long before we hit Loveland thirty-five miles in, neither of us could sit down.

"My ass has never hurt this bad!" I shouted over the noise of the passing cars and vicious crosswind. "This sucks more than anything has ever sucked before!" Tim shouted back in his best Beavis and Butthead impersonation.

We must have looked like two of the biggest dorks to ever ride bikes. Tim had on a black baseball cap and red tank top. I had my hat on backward and wore a sleeveless shirt. Both of us were wearing running shorts and rode standing up the whole time. When we finally arrived at his parents' house, it had been three hours and twenty minutes of torture since we had set out. We passionately agreed that biking sucked and that after this day, we would go back to our bike-less existence.

Upon seeing our sunburned bodies and hearing about our bruised and blistered behinds, Tim's mom went into mother mode.

"Your dad can throw your bikes into the back of the truck and take you back to Boulder," she offered.

We hadn't thought far enough ahead to consider how we were going to get back. Nor had we thought far enough ahead to bring a change of clothes with us to get out of the sweat-soaked ones we were wearing.

Tim looked at me with a mischievous smirk and said, "You know what we would do if we were real men?"

I died a little bit inside, but I could not lose this testosterone-fueled battle. I called Tim's bluff and raised the stakes. "If we were real men, we would ride back to Boulder, and if we don't make it in under three hours, then we have to do it again tomorrow!"

From this point, there was no turning back. Both of us knew the fate that lay ahead. Fortunately, Tim's parents talked us into staying the night, because we didn't have bike lights and it would be dark before we could get back.

The next morning, our bodies ached and our butts were so tender that even sitting on a cushioned couch was painful. Tim's mom had washed our clothes, but we decided that we had better get in a quick ten-mile run before we rode back, because we would be in rough shape to attempt a run later. The run was horrible, like an hour in a torture chamber, but we got it in. Then came the return ride.

As we hit the home stretch between Longmont and Boulder, we looked at the watch and realized that it was going to be close. Both of us knew for certain that if we did not make it back in under three hours, we would hold ourselves to our pledge to do it again the next day. This was *not* an option.

What followed was one of the greatest performances in either of our athletic careers. Like men possessed, we churned the pedals with demonic compulsion. The Diagonal Highway is popular with the large cycling population of Boulder County, so we were not alone on this road. What must have been going through the minds of the groups of cyclists on their expensive road bikes, wearing all the right gear and helmets, as these two skinny distance runners riding cheap mountain bikes went rolling past them? We did not wave. We did not have the breath to utter the polite "On your left" courtesy of passing cyclists. We had tunnel vision fueled by the terror of having to repeat this journey tomorrow. We were in our own world and not at all happy about it.

Legs burning, bottoms blistered and chaffed, and bodies revolting, we pumped up the final hill on Table Mesa Drive. We flung our bikes onto the front lawn of Tim's house and collapsed in exhaustion. Neither of us had the strength or courage to look at the watch. When we finally took a peek at the time and saw 2:52 on the display, we began laughing out loud, high-fiving, and giving ourselves way too much credit for being men.

"You know what I never need to do again?" Tim asked.

"Ride your bike to Fort Collins?" I replied.

"You said it! . . . So where do you want to run tomorrow?"

The desire to do hard things is not limited to runners. It is a human desire that infiltrates almost every population. Video gamers want to blast through Halo on the Legendary mode. Why? Because it is hard! Puzzle aficionados want to complete a five-thousand-piece puzzle because it is hard. Children across the country get out their shovels and begin digging in earnest, believing that if they dig long enough, they will reach China. Why? Because it is hard!

People like to do things just to see if they can. The desire to face our own limitations, overcome obstacles, and finally accomplish what we could not manage previously takes a myriad of forms, from wanting to solve a Rubik's Cube to ordering the spiciest food on the menu and trying to finish it without the assistance of water. The harder the challenge or the more difficult the obstacle, the smaller the number of people who have what it takes to succeed, the greater the feeling of personal satisfaction gained from doing it.

> If you are a good athlete, you tend to thrive on a challenge.
>
> For me, things like injuries are a challenge as something I need to overcome. When I was injured, I used to go to Left Hand Canyon in Boulder and do time trial bike rides just to see how good I could ride it. I loved passing the other riders, and I got down to sixty-six minutes, which some guy told me was maybe one category below professional. That was fun.
>
> **–Dathan Ritzenhein**

Easy things do not hold the same appeal. Imagine if that summer day in Colorado, one of us had said to the other, "I wonder if I could ride my bike all the way to campus and back." That three-mile journey would hold no appeal for us and would not have prompted us to dust off the bikes to try. But riding a distance we had never attempted, where there was a real possibility of failure, was extremely enticing to both of us. In a way, this is similar to running the edge. The act of challenging yourself fulfills the human need to discover what you are capable of and to realize your maximum potential.

THE NIGHT I DIED

Tim

The beginning of the school year in Dubai was always beyond hot. In the four years I taught high school there, I was fortunate to always live in a building with a swimming pool on the roof. At night, when the temperature would cool off to ninety-five degrees, the other teachers and I would venture onto the roof to swim, relax, and socialize with one another.

One night, as I climbed the steps to the roof, I saw my friends Scott and Sophia congratulating each other on becoming the founding members of the UW3 club. They knew I liked to swim and invited me to join. All I had to do to become a member of UW3 was to swim three lengths of the fifteen-meter pool underwater without coming up for air. This sounded like a fun challenge to me. As a former competitive swimmer and fairly fit human, I liked my chances. I made the three laps on my first try, although not without some discomfort. It was not long before we were stretching our limits and taking aim at UW4. Why would we do such a thing? Just to see if we could. A few nights later, all three of us managed to complete four laps. The pain was intense in the last few strokes to reach the wall, but we all pushed through and decided that UW4 was as far as we would ever go.

Without informing one another, Scott and I each began to sneak up to the roof to practice underwater swimming. Both of us believed that UW5 was possible with some training, but did not want the other to know what we were doing.

The next time we were on the roof together, I announced that I was going for it. I stood against the wall and hyperventilated, trying to saturate my lungs with oxygen for the attempt. When I

I am needle phobic, and I got a tattoo. I chickened out when I was eighteen, and then again in college. I am so scared of needles, I have passed out several times, but after the Olympics, I decided to get the rings.

—Amy Yoder Begley

My family has a cabin on a lake in Canada. It is a big lake with an island maybe four hundred meters off the shore and maybe a mile and a half around. One day when I was up there, I decided to swim from our cabin, around the island, and back, just because I wanted to see if I could do it. Down the road, I can't wait to do stuff like that with my kids all the time!

—Alan Webb

reached UW4 and made the turn for UW5, I was in so much pain, I thought my lungs were going to implode. After what seemed like an eternity, I reached the wall and came up for air with a wide-eyed gasp. I threw myself on the side of the pool and continued to wheeze, choke, and fight for air. For several minutes, I thought I might have damaged myself and could feel the veins still bulging in my forehead. When the pain finally subsided, I smiled and basked in UW5 glory. I had done the impossible. I had pushed myself to the absolute limit and felt euphoric with the accomplishment.

Now it was on, and Scott knew he had to respond. After several days of trying, he finally reached the end of UW5 red-faced, writhing in pain, but still able to display a twisted half smile, half grimace of accomplishment. This now exclusive club of two continued to reattempt UW5, but neither of us could repeat the accomplishment. But each of us continued to train when no one else was at the pool. One evening, Scott and Sophia were in the pool while I conversed with them in my street clothes, enjoying the cooler night air. Suddenly, Scott did the unthinkable. He not only completed UW5 for the second time ever, but also pushed off the wall for UW6! In all my years, I have never seen another man in as much pain, so desperate for air, so greedily gulping every molecule of oxygen, when he reached the UW6 wall. He had done it! When he had finally recovered, he recounted that even upon surfacing, he was not sure he was going to live. The fresh air filling his lungs was not aiding his recovery. A few minutes later, he was so full of life as he told the story, wide awake with a light in his eyes shining with a brilliance I had never seen before. Scott recalled that at that moment, "I was as alive as I have ever been. It was amazing!"

I quickly ran downstairs to change into my swimsuit. Scott would not hold the UW6 title alone! As I crouched at the end of the pool adjusting my goggles and saturating my lungs with air, I kept telling myself one thing: "You will not surface until you have reached UW6. No matter what occurs, or how desperate you feel, you will not surface!"

The first four laps underwater hurt with an intensity eclipsing my previous attempt. When I finally reached the wall at the end of the fifth length, I could feel my eyes protruding from my skull. My lungs felt like a vacuum cleaner stuck on a flat object, sucking for all they were worth but getting no air. Still I made the turn and pushed off for my sixth lap. *You will not surface!*

That thought is the last thing I remember. The rest of this story I will have to reconstruct from what Scott and Sophia described. Apparently, not only did I reach the wall for UW6, but I turned and pushed off for UW7. Then my body went limp and I began to sink. I believe I had lost consciousness somewhere during that sixth length of the pool, but my body continued to execute its last command.

At first, Scott laughed while my body sank, thinking I was joking. Then, he quickly realized I was in no state to joke. He jumped into the pool and pulled me to the surface.

The first thing I remember was waking up in Scott's arms feeling as if I had been asleep for eight hours. I was completely confused and disoriented, not knowing where I was and wondering why I was in a pool and, more importantly, why Scott was holding me under the arms. He began to laugh, and Sophia followed. Their relief that I was alive manifested in hysterical laughter and excited accounts of what had just happened. It was several minutes before I could separate the surreal dream world from reality and days before I was able to fully process that if I had been alone and training for this contest, I would have drowned.

Scott and I agreed that this was the end of the UW club. There would be no more attempts. Where we disagreed was on who held the title. To this day, he does not believe I officially made UW6, because I "did not surface under my own power." I maintain that conscious or not, the fact that I pushed off the wall toward UW7 means that I swam farther underwater than either of us had done before. Either way, both of us were satisfied that we had taken this game as far as it could go.

Mountain climbers are fond of the saying, "Because it's there," when asked why they want to get to the summit. What is their reward other than knowing they did it? If it were easy, it would not be as much fun.

Swimming six laps underwater and riding cheap bikes long distances also hold no extrinsic reward. The appeal rests simply in the great difficulty of these feats. It provides the context we crave in the absence of real life-and-death, fight-or-flight situations. There may be no extrinsic reward, but the feelings of satisfaction, self-worth, and accomplishment are almost always worth the struggle. The harder the better. The fewer who can, the greater the appeal. The closer you must get to your limits to achieve your goal, the greater the feelings of gratification, pride, and fulfillment.

The challenge of this book and in becoming a distance maven will be difficult. It could be, and should be, one of the hardest things you will ever do. Because it is so difficult, the rewards and payoffs will be tremendous!

Running is hard enough all by itself. The drive-by taunters screaming, "Run, Forrest!" as you measure the road one stride at a time do not have what it takes. The millions who know they should run or at least exercise a little to take care of their bodies don't have what it takes. They cannot get off their couches or out the door for more than three consecutive weeks following a New Year's resolution. They cannot climb the mountain.

Just in being a runner, you have already succeeded in doing something many cannot. But to become a distance maven, you will need to demand even more of yourself. You will need to dedicate yourself to a higher set of standards in a quest to become a better runner and better human being. You will continue to challenge yourself by completing interval sessions with an all-time best personal average, getting that elusive PR in a 5K race, and running further and faster than your previous self could, but you will also take a hard look at the difference between your real and ideal self as a runner and as a person. When you do, you will be ready for the hardest challenge of all: to commit to taking the actions necessary to create an ideal version of yourself and to live an extraordinary life as a distance maven.

WAY of the MAVEN

What Have You Done?

The next step in becoming a distance maven is to take stock of all the hard things you already do or have already done. Write a list, beginning with running. Start with your longest or hardest runs and races. Include your fastest times or best performances. Then think beyond running, and look for other activities, interests, or accomplishments you have had in your life. Put these accomplishments in another list.

These two lists will serve as your own personal examples for the distance maven attributes we will outline in Part 2. Spend a little time on these tasks and come up with at least five difficult things you have accomplished in running, and five in life outside of running.

You can add to the lists as you read the book or even long after you've finished reading it. As a distance maven, you will find yourself continually drawn to hard things and choosing challenges that allow you to test your limits.

CHAPTER 5

The Curse of Normal and the Chains of Average

> Gather ye rosebuds while ye may,
> Old Time is still a-flying:
> And this same flower that smiles to-day
> To-morrow will be dying.
> —Robert Herrick, 1591-1674

Distance mavens may possess great courage in races, in workouts, or in facing and overcoming their own imperfections, but one thing fills them with a fear too great to even contemplate: wasted potential. Because they now see themselves with greater clarity and know where their true potential lies, the thought of wasting these talents is almost too much to bear. They are petrified of living a normal life that does not challenge them to become more. A life that does not portray or represent their maximum capability is unthinkably scary. To be trapped in a normal or average life, where they are not able to self-actualize and become the person they are meant to be, would be the cruelest of fates.

Tim

I graduated from high school in 1990 as part of the centennial class from Fort Collins High School. One hundred years' worth of graduates had participated in this same ritual before me. Although I had the majority of my life in front of me, I was almost certain that every member of that first graduating class was now dead. This thought had been haunting me since I saw the film *Dead Poets Society* over the summer heading into my senior year.

In the movie, English teacher John Keating (Robin Williams) recites Robert Herrick's "Gather ye rosebuds" poem in an attempt to inspire his young students to contemplate their own mortality. On the first day of school, he takes his students into the hallway to have them look at pictures of students from the early days in the school's history. What each of these people has in common, explains Keating, is that they are all "fertilizing daffodils." He implores his students to imagine the advice these dead classmates might give them. Should the present students wait and let life happen to them, hoping for the best? Or should they seize the day? The Latin phrase *carpe diem* becomes the motto of the movie as the students vow to live life to its fullest, or as Thoreau recommends, "to live deliberately . . . and not, when I came to die, discover that I had not lived . . . I wanted to live deep and suck out all the marrow of life."

The movie had a great impact on me. Like the students in the movie, I vowed not to live passively. I wanted desperately to live an extraordinary life. But wanting to do something and actually doing it are very different things.

CARPE DIEM! CARPE VIAM! DEAD POETS AND RUNNERS

The truth is that we will all die one day, or as Williams's character put it, we are all "food for worms." This life is our only shot. It is not a practice round, and we do not get a second chance. Two inescapable facts greet us every day that we are lucky enough to wake up. First, someday we will die. And second, we are not dead yet. The distance between now and when we die may not be up to us, but what we do between now and then is in our control. Should we play it safe, take the easy road, and do just enough to get by? Should we spend our days in idle pursuits waiting for our end point to come? Or should we "suck out all the marrow of life" and seize the day?

The worldwide organization known as the Dead Runners Society has taken inspiration from the movie as well and created a community of runners known as Deads, who meet up at races and even hold world conferences. They have changed *carpe diem* to *carpe viam*, claiming to "seize the road," or, in more direct translation, "seize the way." Runners are examples of people who have already chosen a unique path. They have already decided to live actively, to get out the door and do something rather than doing nothing. So the marriage between the philosophy in the movie and the mind-set of a runner is a good one. Seizing the way is exactly what this book and becoming a distance maven are about. The way is found on the edge of what is possible and an unrelenting quest for peak performance both in running and in life.

> I have my days when I wonder why I am doing this. I feel like it is one step forward and two steps back, but I just keep going.
>
> **—Kara Goucher**

NO TIME TO KILL

Adam

I have a few recurring theme songs in my life. When I need to refocus on who I am and what I am about, I can listen to these songs and be reminded of what is important. One song that has been at the top of my playlist for years is "No Time to Kill," by Clint Black and Hayden Nicholas. They put a country slant on the *carpe diem* motto:

> *The highest cost of livin's dyin', that's one everybody pays*
> *So have it spent before you get the bill, there's no time to kill.*

You might recognize this sentiment from the last chapter and how Tim and I dislike the word *someday* and the phrase *I have always wanted to*. There is no telling how many somedays we have left, so whenever possible, someday should be today. The other option is, as Clint Black sings, to "keep killin' time until . . . there's no time to kill."

Nothing brought the importance of this philosophy home to me more than the death of cross-country teammate Chris Severy in 1998, my senior year at University of Colorado. As chronicled by Chris Lear in *Running with the Buffaloes*, a book about the university's men's cross-country team, Chris was a bright light. He was smart, caring, and talented. His future was perhaps the brightest I have ever seen. He was one of those rare people who seemed to have no limits. "Most likely to succeed someday" was an understatement for someone as remarkable as Chris. When he lost control of his bike coming down Flagstaff Mountain and collided with a tree, a light went out. All of his tomorrows and somedays became irrelevant. The world lost a better future without Chris in it. For Chris, there was no more time to kill. For the rest of us, left with his loss, we had to learn from this harsh lesson and had to change how we looked at our remaining days.

I know that Chris did not wake up on that October morning thinking it might be his last. This is not how life works. I have no idea when my days will run out, but between now and that time, I am determined not to settle for average, normal, or good enough.

There is nothing wrong with being a normal person who lives an average life. In fact, it is a far easier road than the one we propose, but when you lace up your shoes and head out the front door, you have already separated yourself from a normal life. The moment you begin to swing your arms and place one foot in front of another, you have entered an exceptional world filled with exceptional people. For at least the time you are out on the track, trails, or roads, you are the opposite of normal.

If runners are already abnormal, distance mavens are even more so. Distance mavens possess the awareness and ability to spill that hour of exceptional living during a run into the remaining hours of their day. Excellence in everything means to live an extraordinary existence not only in the running sphere but also in the entire amphitheater of life. In no aspect of life do mavens wish to be ordinary or to settle for average. In how they do ordinary, day-to-day tasks such as mowing the lawn, relate to their families and friends, or go about their work, distance mavens are compelled to do each of these things better today than they have ever done them before. *Carpe diem* and *carpe viam*. Seize the day by seizing the way of the distance maven.

WEIRDOS, FREAKS, AND BREAKING THE MOLD

As a runner, you have no doubt come across other runners who make eccentric people look normal. Perhaps you are this runner. The social oddity, the maverick, the proverbial square peg in a round hole, the freak, and the screwball tend to feel comfortable in the runner's skin. Some people would claim that they would need to have a couple screws loose to even try distance running (and perhaps they are right), but what an outsider might consider a weakness is actually one of the runner's greatest strengths. Runners give each other permission to be themselves. Ultimately, no one is as normal as he or she seems, but runners don't have to hide it. Think about your best friends. Did you know they were this strange and had this many idiosyncrasies when you first met them? More likely than not, as you grew to know each other better, you each revealed the freak inside, knowing you would not be judged. For the most part, the running world accepts its strangest members as valuable citizens. The common bond

My teammates are like my brothers. We completely, one hundred percent, hold each other accountable. We push each other when we need it, and we knock each other down when we need it and pick each other up when something goes wrong or somebody has a bad day.

—Chris Solinsky

and understanding between them as runners is more powerful than condescending judgments based on a few quirks.

Tim

During one of my years coaching high school, two freshmen girls came out for the cross-country team full of energy and spirit. The second day of practice, I could not remember either of their names, so I just called out to them as "Freak 1" and "Freak 2." They smiled and giggled, but I could tell they did not know what to make of these labels. When they asked me after practice why I called them freaks instead of Maryanne and Becky, I told them that freshmen did not deserve real names because they were not yet real people. Even more confusion was scribbled across their faces, so I continued, "Normal people are boring, and I would much rather spend my time around people who are strange and interesting. You two seem like cool freaks to me. You are freaks, right?"

They looked at each other and broke into wide smiles. "We are not just freaks, we are superfreaks!"

The next week, they came to practice wearing matching shirts that read "Freak 1" and "Freak 2" across the back. For the rest of the year, if I ever called them by their real names, they were quick to correct me. I was right in what I told them. They were much more fun to be around than any normal person would have been.

How does any of this translate into aspects of life beyond running? Consider the following business example.

SOMETHING'S FISHY

In 1986, the Pike Place Fish Market in Seattle was on the verge of bankruptcy. A normal fish market doing normal business, Pike Place was failing in a very normal way. The market had two choices: It could do the normal thing and accept its fate, or it could break free from the chains of normal and do something unusual to save the business.

How the market turned around its fortunes is well documented. It decided to become "world famous" and, more importantly, to have as much fun as possible in the fish-selling business. Buying a fish from the Pike Place Fish Market became an event. Unsuspecting fish buyers expecting a normal fish-buying experience, where they select a fish and the polite employee wrapped it up for them, collected their money, and wished them a nice day, were in for a surprise. What greeted the fish buyers instead were the happiest, the most energetic, and probably the strangest employees they had ever seen. The workers began chanting orders, loudly bantering back and forth with each other and entertaining the customer. Now, when a customer orders a fish, the seller shouts out the order. The rest of the staff shouts the order in unison before the newly purchased fish is launched across the stand and into the waiting arms of another worker. They will even let the fish buyer hurl the fish if the customer wishes. The order is wrapped up with flair and celebration. Every sale is like a mini party. The staff's act expanded and quickly revitalized the company as Pike Place enjoyed a wild ride to achieving its goal of becoming world famous. Pike Place Fish Market has since been featured on television shows, in business training seminars and on a host of YouTube videos, where you can see the mayhem for yourself. In the summer months, the fish market is a popular tourist destination and can attract up to ten thousand visitors a day. It was also voted by CNN as one of the most fun places to work in America.

By breaking the mold and becoming a fish market oddity, Pike Place Fish Market was no longer a normal place to buy fish or a normal place to work. It had broken the curse and become exceptional.

Raise your hand if either now or in the future, you would like to be an exceptional parent. Keep your hand in the air if you would love to build exceptional friendships with all the important people in your life. How about being an exceptional runner? Neighbor? Employee? Boss? Student? Part of the commitment of the distance maven is that you wish to become excellent and extraordinary at everything. Most likely every human on earth would like to achieve excellence in everything, but the distance maven takes steps to make it happen.

Running is not easy. If it were, it would lack its appeal. But you are a runner. You are doing something most people cannot do. You are already exceptional. It does not matter how fast you are, how you place in your age group, or how many miles you run a week. Still, could you be a better runner? Could you take your running to a higher level and shatter your personal goals? Hopefully, you answered yes to those questions. In the following chapters, we will be looking at how you can become a better runner. But for now, let's assume that you are a runner and that this observation alone means you are living at least one aspect of your life on the edge, striving for improvement and discovering your potential. It takes work to be a runner. It takes consistent action. Sitting on the couch, wishing to be a runner, will not get you there.

Likewise, in your other life stories, you will have to take action to be exceptional. It will require work, discipline, initiative, and focus. You will need to become aware of the role you play in each of your life stories and take heroic action to improve.

Why would anyone want to do this? Because it is hard and because you want to break the curse of "normal" and the chains of "average." When should you begin? Today! Because someday may never come.

THE FIVE LIFE STORIES

The next steps we need to take in becoming distance mavens is to identify areas of our lives in which we have accepted normal or have fallen into a less-than-exceptional rut. We need to look closely at each of our five life stories and identify where we have settled for average instead of maximizing our potential for success. If we could design our lives from the outside, which of our stories would we discover are not living up to our highest standards and which stories would we change?

We don't need to have all the solutions at this time, but this list will help us identify which parts of our lives we want to work on and improve. Let's again consider the five life stories one at a time.

As you go through your stories, reflect on your real level of success versus your ideal level of success. Are they the same, or is there a large gap between them? Consider what you have settled for. Make a list of areas you would like to improve upon. This list will be different for every reader and can change over time. Make your list as honest and complete as possible so that you will have plenty to work on in Part 2.

Education. Maybe you are still in school, or maybe you are finished. Either way, your education is not complete. The conventional measures of educational success are grades, college acceptances, and degrees, but long after you complete your formal schooling, you must continue to learn. You must be a student of changing technologies, social trends, and even pop culture. The world will not stop changing just because you have finished school. When you start a new job, you will have to learn new systems, policies, and procedures. You might start a family, which would require you to learn how to change diapers, negotiate bedtimes, and offer timely advice. This list could go on, but you get the point. You and everyone else are all students in one way or another. As soon as you stop learning, you stop growing.

Career. If you are still in school, you might not have begun your career yet, but maybe you have a job or at least chores to do at home. If you are in the middle of a career, is it satisfying? Are you doing all you can to be exceptional? Do you brighten the day of your coworkers or bring them down? Are you dedicated to being the best at whatever task or service you provide? Where could you improve in your career life story? What would your career look like if you could design the absolute ideal?

Friendships. Think about your closest friends as well as your more casual acquaintances. Do they all know how you value them? Do you communicate and put in the work necessary to maintain close relationships? Do you take them for granted and settle for good enough? Could you be a better friend, an exceptional friend? Build stronger relationships? Repair broken relationships with important people?

Family. We play many roles in our family life stories. Sons, daughters, fathers, mothers, brothers, sisters, cousins, grandparents, uncles, and aunts. Each of these roles is important, and how you play your roles has a great influence on the family as a whole. This is one life story all of us could likely improve. Think about your roles. Think about the relationships you have with your family members. Which relationships could be improved if you worked on them? How do the roles you play in your family serve to create the best dynamic possible?

> I got into the competitive endurance sports because I enjoyed relying on myself more than relying on a team and it allowed me to discover my limits and find out characteristics about myself that were good. Sometimes I find bad ones, too, but those are lessons you can take with you into other aspects of your life.
>
> **—Dathan Ritzenhein**

Passions. Start with running, and consider if you are getting all you want and need out of this passion. What could improve? Then move on to your other passions, and consider them the same way. Maybe you enjoy cooking or needlepoint work. Maybe you enjoy building things out of wood or writing blogs. Maybe you are involved in your church or a social club. No matter what your interests and passions are, do you believe you are getting all you can out of them?

THE BOILING FROG

Think back to when you were a teenager. If you are a teenager, this will not be very difficult! Now imagine that a guest speaker comes into one of your tenth-grade classes and passes out the following checklist. Nod your head yes for each of the following statements that apply to you.

- I would like to graduate from high school with good grades.
- I would like to get into a good university of my choice.
- If I go to university, I would like to be a successful student and earn a degree.
- When I am done with school, I would like to get a good job I enjoy doing.
- I would like to be successful in my work and earn several promotions as I climb the career ladder.
- I would like to have a husband or wife someday.
- I would like my marriage to be loving, faithful, and caring and to last forever.
- I would like to have children someday.
- If I have children, I would like to be an amazing mother or father to my children and form intimate, caring, and stable relationships with them.
- I would like my life to be full of meaningful and lasting friendships.
- I would like to have several pastimes to pursue to bring balance and diversity to my life.
- I would like to do more good in the world than bad.
- I would like to be happy for the majority of my life, and when I die, I would like to be filled with contentment and satisfaction that my life was important.

Each of the five life stories is represented in the list above, and more likely than not, you were nodding yes to the majority of the statements. You would be hard pressed to find a teenager or any other person who does not wish for these basic levels of success and happiness or who does not wish his or her life to matter.

When we ask groups of young people a series of questions much like the ones above, there is almost universal agreement and optimism for each statement. We always follow up these questions with this question: "Do you believe that you will be successful in each of these areas as an adult?" Again, we get almost all affirmative responses.

Here is where it gets interesting. We next follow with this list of questions:

- Do you know an adult who was not very good in school or who did not get into a university he or she desired?
- Do you know an adult who has been unsuccessful in a career or even unable to hold down a job?
- Do you know an adult who is, or has been, in a bad marriage?
- Do you know an adult who is a bad husband, wife, father, or mother?
- Do you know an adult who has difficulty making or keeping friends?
- Do you believe that these same adults whom you were just thinking of in the previous questions believed they would be successful in each of these areas when they were your age?

Somewhere between the optimism of youth and the reality of adulthood, there is a breakdown. Sadly, many adults fail to achieve even an average life. They are shackled by the chains of incompetence long before they experience the curse of normal. What causes this breakdown? How do people allow themselves to create lives that do not live up to their own hopes and aspirations?

If teenagers could look forward ten or fifteen years and see what will become of their lives, there might well be massive panic, followed by intense efforts to prevent themselves from creating lives that do not match their youthful optimism. If adults could go back to those formative years and do it all over again, they would probably avoid the pit-falls and take the actions necessary to create more satisfying lives.

The problem is that over a ten- or fifteen-year span, we allow our-selves to very slowly settle for less than our ideal. Just a little less effort here and a little less determination there adds up over the years to a very average life. It is much like the story of the boiling frog.

The premise of the story goes like this: If you place a frog into hot or even very warm water, the frog will hop, jump, and struggle to get out. But if you place the frog into room-temperature water like that of a pond, it will sit comfortably, as frogs do. If you suddenly raise the water temperature, the frog will again try to escape. If, however, you increase the temperature very slowly, the frog will not notice the change until it is too late and will die smiling, never even thinking to escape.

Accurate or not, the notion of the boiling frog is useful in under-standing how slow change does not have the same impact that quick change would have. The slow descent into an average and unfulfilling life goes by unnoticed. Like the slowly rising water temperature, it is not enough to cause alarm or even concern. When a situation in one of our life stories gets to the boiling point, we are finally forced to take action and try to escape. A failing marriage, a dead-end job, a broken friendship, stagnant or dormant passions—all these problems reveal the gap between the life we believed we would live and the life we ac-tually have.

Distance mavens don't need to worry about becoming boiled frogs. In Part 2, we will learn how running and following the path of the maven not only can make us acutely aware of the water temperature around us, but can also arm us with the tools necessary to escape the curse of a normal life and break free from the chains of average.

PART 2
The Six Mirrors

If you run, you are a runner. It doesn't matter how fast or how far. It doesn't matter if today is your first day or if you've been running for twenty years. There is no test to pass, no license to earn, no membership card to get. You just run.

—**John Bingham**

Before we can change who we are, we must be acutely aware of who we are. If you had a car that was not running well, would you open the hood and begin tinkering with wires, adjusting screws, and replacing parts without a solid understanding of what each wire, screw, and part was made to do? How about a computer? If it slowed down or developed other problems, would you feel comfortable opening up registry files, changing settings, deleting applications, and making other changes in the hope that you would fix your computer?

In the car and computer examples, you recognize a problem. The machines are not performing at the level you would like. You know that changes need to be made, but you would not begin making those changes without first understanding the nature of this particular car or computer and its issues.

In Part 1, you identified some areas of your life that you thought could be raised to a higher level. You identified attributes you would like to possess and envisioned how each of your life stories could be improved. Most importantly, you committed to follow the way of the distance maven, which reflects your desire to improve your life by constantly striving to get closer to your ideal version of yourself.

To clarify what we meant by improving our lives, in Part 1 we differentiated between five life stories in which we can be successful and find fulfillment. We also discussed the idea of the self and defined it as the qualities that make us who we are—the qualities that lead to our individual ways of behaving, thinking, and perceiving the world.

Several Greek philosophers, including Socrates, have been credited with the phrase "Know thyself." Although the true origin of this phrase is in doubt, the wisdom behind it is not. Knowing ourselves seems like a simple task, since we spend every minute of every day with ourselves, but very few people take the time to get to know themselves on a deeper level. Distance mavens are experts in self-knowledge. Armed with keen insight, distance mavens see themselves with clarity and realism. In the next six chapters, we will take the time to examine ourselves. We will take a long and perhaps difficult look at ourselves in six mirrors, each reflecting an aspect of ourselves to reveal who we really are.

By analyzing our reflections in these six mirrors, we will identify the aspects of ourselves, both in our running and in our other life stories, that are underperforming. Like the auto mechanic and computer technician, we will become experts, not only able to detect the precise areas that need attention but also able to understand the nature of the issue to fix and improve our overall performance. By the time we are finished examining our reflections in each of the six mirrors, we will be empowered not only to discover ourselves, but to create better versions of ourselves according to our own design. This is the way of the distance maven.

ACTORS AND REACTORS

A hammer can do nothing on its own. It is a tool, an instrument or a device that must be used and manipulated by a builder to have an effect. A puppet without a puppeteer is also a tool, an inanimate object waiting for a hand to give it life and purpose. Hammers and puppets are reactors, while the builder and the puppeteer are actors. By *actor*, we mean a doer—someone who purposefully acts to achieve a goal. In our lives, we can either be actors or reactors. Reactors have no vision or direction of their own. Like tools, they react according to the whims of the hands directing them. Without much thought or awareness, they are often shocked and disappointed with the lives they find themselves living. As victims of circumstance and tools of the situation, many of these people don't realize that they are capable of being the actors directing and building the lives they want to live. Distance mavens are actors, runners in pursuit of better lives through thoughtful action.

The mission to rise up and overthrow our own mediocrity means we must reject the idea of being reactors like the hammer or puppet and become actors like the builder or puppeteer to create excellence in our five life stories. As runners, we learn valuable lessons about ourselves and our capabilities. These lessons can provide the awareness and vision we need to be actors, distance mavens creating our personal revolutions.

Because you are a runner, you already know what it is like to be the actor in charge of your running life story, working hard in a consistent direction to achieve your goals. Consider the following example. When the alarm clock cuts through the morning before the sun has even bothered to rise above the horizon, when the weather is cold and the wind is blowing, when your body aches from yesterday's workout and begs you for a day off, these are the times when you as a runner are faced with temptations and when stepping out the front door seems like a terrible idea. The easy road tempts you. The urge to choose inaction over action is strong. Your lofty goals of setting new personal records or running that first marathon don't seem as important. One more day off to sleep in a little, to wait for better weather, or to let the sore muscles recover seems like a great idea. It would be easier to allow yourself to react to the situation by sitting back and allowing yourself to be manipulated by circumstance.

But as a hard-core runner, you crawl out of bed anyway. You lace up your shoes and put on just enough clothing to protect yourself from the elements. You step out the door and begin to put one foot in front of the other. You know that as bad an idea as this run seems right now, by the time it is over, you will be rewarded with a deep satisfaction and the peace of mind that you got the run in. You are in control of your life. You are the puppeteer instead of the puppet. Because you are creating your running story one day at a time through your decisions and actions, you are directing your life rather than allowing it to direct you. You are creating the life you want to live.

You could have allowed the early hour to coax you into choosing another hour of sleep. You could have allowed the harsh weather to keep you indoors. You could have allowed your sore calves from yesterday's track session to talk you into resting and relaxing. All of these choices would have meant that you were a tool of circumstance, allowing weather, chance, and whim to make your decisions for you.

In each of our life stories, we have a similar paradigm. We can choose to be the directors of our own lives by taking the actions necessary to create the life we want to live, or we can sit back and wait for our lives to happen to us and then react. Reactors might want to be successful, but they are unaware of what it takes or the role they play in their own success and failure. They might want their lives to improve, but do not know where to begin or which direction to follow.

Distance mavens strive to become more aware of themselves and the role they play in their own success. This awareness gives them direction and allows them to take action toward consistent self-improvement and to creating the life they wish to live.

The distance-maven ruler pictured here symbolizes the way of the maven versus the way of the reactor. In the next six chapters, as we use six mirrors to gain further insight into who we really are, this ruler will allow us to chart the positive attributes we learn from running and how we can apply them to each of our life stories.

Like most gauges, the ends represent the extremes. Very few of us will fall on either extreme, but understanding each end of the gauge helps us better understand the middle. And somewhere in the middle is where most of us fit, although we may lean to the left in some areas and to the right in others. Most people never take the time to look in the mirror and accurately assess their strengths and limitations. But to be true to the commitment of the distance maven, we must become self-aware enough to understand ourselves and where we fall on this line, and then we must take the necessary steps and actions to move ourselves further to the right—closer to our ideal and closer to the edge of what is possible.

CHAPTER 6

Get off the Couch

INITIATIVE

What if Superman were lazy? What if he could not get himself off the couch and away from the TV long enough to use his superpowers? It would not matter what he could do or how many superpowers he possessed; he would not be a hero. He would be unable to defeat the very first villain he encountered: his own lack of initiative.

To be a hero requires action. First and foremost, all heroes must be proactive and possess a strong drive to do, to act, to execute, to try. Without the capacity for action, heroes would live passive lives and no one would ever know who the heroes were or what they could have accomplished. They would be reactors watching life happen. For the runner, initiative can come and go. At times, we are full of optimism and confidence, which propel us to run and work out. At other times, even the most motivated runners can get into a slump. "I feel like running," says former Olympian Nick Rogers, "but that does not necessarily translate into getting me off the couch, and out the front door." These words may sound surprising coming from a guy who reached the highest level of competition this sport has to offer, but his sentiments are not surprising. Nick has a blossoming new career, a wife, and a new baby at home. His priorities have shifted, and in his current position, he is having trouble being motivated to run every day. Most runners battle this ebb and flow of motivation at many points in their careers.

> There have been peaks and valleys in my motivation. . . . Even in a single week, there are ups and downs, but even when I have been injured, the overall motivation to run drives me. It is like being in love with someone. There are ups and downs, but the love is always there; it is just in you.
>
> **–Alan Webb**

Before we look at the solution, let's look deeper into the problem. Without initiative, or the capacity to act, to make things happen or just to *do something*, we run the risk of living passive lives waiting for things to happen. We wait for opportunities instead of making them. We wait for love, for our big break, for a problem to disappear. We are waiting for our lives to live us, instead of going out and living our lives with purpose and action.

Without initiative, Superman would just be a man in a tight blue suit and someone whom people would laugh at as they tried to step on his cape. He would be a reactor, not a hero, because he would never do anything heroic. You still might want to avoid him in a bar fight, but his life would be more comical than fit for comic books and movies.

TWO YEARS IN A LIFE

Imagine that the next 365 days of your life starts right now, in this very moment. Now imagine that someone gives you two options on how to live the next year of your life.

Option 1

For the next 365 days, you will live your life passively. You will do what needs to be done: show up to school or work, pay the bills, take out the trash, get your annual physical, take your two weeks' vacation, send all the right birthday cards and Christmas letters, fix what breaks, buy what needs replacing, cook your favorite foods, eat at your favorite restaurants, hang out with your friends, enjoy your romantic and family relationships, and do all the other things normal people do. You will not go out of your way to do anything that requires more than what is necessary. It will not be a bad year. It will be a safe year, a good year, a normal year. When it is all over, 365 days from right now, you get to look back on a year of your life that you will never be able to live again. How much of it will you remember? How many of those 365 days will stick out in your memory? How many stories will you have? No doubt, you will have some memories, but most likely, these memories will be things that happened to you, not things you made happen. We would argue that the number of days you can remember out of those 365 days is the number of days you actually lived. The rest of the days—those that blend into oblivion—are lost forever without a memory or story to make them significant enough to matter.

Option 2

For the next 365 days, you will live actively. You will still do what needs to be done, go to work, pay the bills, and tend to all those other everyday aspects of normal living. In addition, and depending on where you are in life, you will also do some extra and even extraordinary things. The nature of these extra things will, of course, depend on your marital status, whether you have children, the nature of your job, your economic situation, your age, and myriad other factors, but the concept remains the same. Look at these examples, and apply them to your particular situation.

This year, you do something that you have never done before in running. You sign up for your first marathon, your first triathlon, or perhaps an ultra. You will need to train harder than ever to get ready for it. Maybe you join a new training group or begin some ancillary training like yoga or Pilates. You will also do several spontaneous and mildly crazy things with your friends. Maybe you will load up the car and head out for a weekend road trip to Las Vegas, driving through the night Sunday to be back in time for Monday morning. You will stretch yourself in another passion you have been putting off, like signing up for private foreign-language lessons or learning to play the trumpet. In your relationships, you will ask out the person you have been staring at from across the room for the last two months, or you will throw your partner a surprise party for no reason at all. You will take more risks, say yes to more opportunities, and seek out new experiences.

> I have seen a lot of people come and go because they lack motivation. For me, looking back at the moments that are really special helps [me] define the next goal. I have been frustrated about the amount of cross-training I had to do. But then, when things start going again, it makes it all worth it. When you stop having goals is when your motivation is done.
>
> **–Dathan Ritzenhein**

Not all of these extra things will go well. You might crash from dehydration during your triathlon or ultra, get a speeding ticket on the way back from Vegas, make a fool of yourself at your first trumpet recital, or be thoroughly rejected by that person you asked out. Some risks will pay off with great rewards, and others will allow you to crash and burn. Either way, you will still be creating stories and memories that you would not have had if you hadn't taken those risks. It will not be safe or normal; it will be exciting and certainly memorable.

Which option would you choose? Which year would you rather live? Safe, normal, pleasant, but forgettable? Or exciting, compelling, maybe dramatic, but certainly memorable? For distance mavens, the choice is easy. Distance mavens always choose action over inaction and are not afraid to take risks to live more exhilarating, rewarding, and distinctive lives. But to live Option 2 requires action, initiative, vision, and optimism.

When we decide to take action, our lives expand. We end up creating the stories and memories that make us interesting to talk to at parties.

BEAR PEAK

Tim

When I was coaching high school, my runners were always asking me to tell them stories about running at the University of Colorado. They wanted to know about our workouts and the hardest runs we did. I told them that the hardest run I knew was Bear Peak. It was a little over an hour of running straight uphill to reach the summit. By the time you reached to the top, you were completely exhausted and still had to come down the other side. As soon as I told the story, several of them asked if they could do it.

I told them they were not yet ready for a run like that, but this only made them want to do it more. Why did they want to do it? If you need an answer to that question, go back and reread Chapter 4. They wanted to do it because I told them that they couldn't and that it was too hard. Still, I refused to take them until one day, they trapped me in my own logic. "You always tell us to challenge our limits. You always tell us to do hard things. You always tell us that we should take action and do things, even things we may not be able to achieve. You tell us to live our lives in a way that we are creating the stories we will tell our children one day. This is a story we want to tell our children! We want to tell them about the day we attempted to run up Bear Peak!" How could I say no now? I agreed to take the varsity-level seniors up the mountain, but they would have to agree to follow my instructions to the letter.

The rules were simple. Because it was a loop, and because I was the only one who knew the way, it was all or nothing. Rule number one was, either we all made it to the summit, or we would all turn around and go back. Rule number two was also based on safety. If we got spread out on the trail, the leaders would stop to regroup with the rest of the team every time there was a fork in the trail, or every ten minutes. This would make sure we did not lose anyone. They agreed to my two simple rules, and on the first weekend of Christmas break, eight eager runners and one naive coach loaded into two cars and made the hour-long drive to Boulder.

On a normal day in the spring or summer, this run is epic. It requires a minimum of sixty minutes of running straight uphill to reach the top. On the December day that we chose to make our attempt, it was very cold and very windy. If I had known just how cold and how dangerous it would become at the top, I would never have gone ahead with our plan.

The run started out fine, with lots of rolling hills and hard breathing. Fifteen minutes in, we reached the base of Bear Canyon and began the long, steady climb to the top. We were over an hour into the run before we could even see the summit. It was still a long way off, we were exhausted, and the wind was getting colder and starting to sting our faces. Our thin running gloves were proving to be no match against the relentless cold. We resorted to shoving our hands into our armpits or down our pants to keep them warm. No one was happy, and I was becoming concerned that if it got much colder, we could be in real danger. Most of us were wearing long-sleeved shirts and shorts along with running hats and thin gloves. We were not carrying water. If we stopped moving for too long, we would quickly freeze. When we regrouped at seventy minutes, I shouted over the wind that we were about thirty minutes from the summit. I recommended that we head back now and call it a day, but left the decision to them. They might have been tempted, but we could see the peak and they wanted to make it to the top. The decision was quickly made to press on. It turned out to be a very bad decision.

Twenty-five minutes later, with numb feet, aching hands, and burning faces, we were taking the last few paces to the rocky summit. The peak was very small, with jagged rocks jutting out in all directions. We enjoyed the view for about five seconds before I started yelling over the wind for them to head back down to the trail. I had to be careful not to let the panic building up inside me show through my actions. I would have given anything in those moments to go back in time and refuse to take them on this run. When we got to the trail leading down the other side, I realized that we were missing Chris. I told everyone to head down the trail, following the same rules as before. I would go back and get Chris, and we would catch up. I was beginning to lose control of my thoughts as terror gripped me from the inside out. I knew we were minutes away from mass hypothermia, and I had to keep everyone moving and get them off this mountain. I crawled around the rocks of the summit, screaming for Chris. I could not even hear my own voice over the wind, which was blowing directly into my face and making it difficult to keep my eyes open. I saw Chris standing on a rock with his back arched, yelling at the sky. He had thrown off his gloves and was clearly out of his mind. I led him off the rocks, but his fingers were unable to bend to climb down. We had to take the long way around the peak and waste more precious time away from the rest of the group. When we finally reached the trail, I implored Chris to run hard so that we could catch the team. Fortunately, running fast was one thing Chris did very well. We flew down the trail and found the team huddled together in a small cave, trying to shield themselves from the wind and absorb each other's body heat. Relieved to have the group together and safe, the fear and anxiety inside me started to dissipate. The trail led us into the trees and away from the howling wind, and we started to thaw a little. It was then that two runners made a decision that almost cost them their lives.

After we left the cave, Nate and Brady ran ahead of the group, but at the next fork in the trail, they were nowhere to be seen. They had apparently taken it upon themselves to find their own way back. I don't know if I was more angry or scared at this point. If they chose the right trails, they would be fine. If they chose wrong . . . I didn't want to think about it.

After three hours and twenty minutes, six weary runners and I made it back to where we had started. Each of us was exhausted beyond anything we had experienced before. I was nervous to see if Nate and Brady were waiting for us. They were nowhere to be found. The alarm and dread that I had felt at the summit paled in comparison with the foreboding terror that washed over me at that moment. I sprinted out and back on several trails, shouting for Nate and Brady, but there were too many options and I did not know where they might be. I had no choice but to call Search and Rescue. It would be dark in less than an hour, and they would not survive the night.

As I was giving their names and last known locations to the police, Chris started yelling at me that they were back! I hung up in relief and ran to meet them. But when I reached the group, I saw that it was only Nate who had returned, and what he told me could have stopped my heart. He said that he had left Brady several miles back when Brady could no longer run more than twenty seconds without stopping to rest. I knew that in his state of fatigue, Nate had lost his reasoning ability, but I wished he had not left Brady alone. After asking Nate to point out the trail he thought Brady might be on, I went sprinting again into the forest. Less than a mile up the trail and just before dusk, I found Brady being escorted by six kind hikers who had found him wandering off trail, delirious and hypothermic. They had draped him in their coats, but his skin was purple and he was unable to shiver. I am not sure why I didn't take him to the hospital to be checked out. He told me he would be OK and just wanted to sit in a hot car and eat.

The heater was on full blast with all vents pointing at Brady sitting cross-legged in the front seat. The three runners in the back were so hot, they had stripped down to shorts and no shirts. The talk turned to the run. Every runner gave his account of the run and agreed that it was absolutely the most challenging thing they had ever done. Nick claimed that at some points, he just wanted to lie down and die up there rather than come down. Brad recalled how he felt as if he could not inhale, because the wind was sucking the air from his chest. Finally, someone asked if it was worth it. Without hesitation, all the boys in the car agreed that it was a great run and that they were glad they had done it. I looked over at Brady, who was finally able to shiver. He grinned at me with a large bite of sandwich in his mouth and said, "That run was awesome!" He said he wanted to do it again when the weather was warmer, but that this time, he would not leave the group.

I pondered silently as the runners continued to share stories. I was aware of how lucky I was that my own poor choices during the run had not been catastrophic. It was easy to blame Nate and Brady for not following directions, but it was my lack of judgment as a coach that put them in a position to make such a choice. As strong as our initiative was to take on this challenge, I should have had the initiative and courage to turn the group around before we ever reached the summit. In Chapter 9, we will discuss the attribute of adaptability and knowing when to bend—an attribute I continue to struggle with and one that would have served me well on this day.

Eight tired runners and one relieved coach made their way back to Denver having lived more in a single day and discovered more about themselves than some people do in a lifetime. They had challenged their limits and overcome adversity. They had run to the edge and then a little further. By taking the initiative to get out the door and do something extraordinary that day, they had lived a story they will one day be telling their grandchildren.

> I was a happy kid, but running made me so much more comfortable in my own skin. The confidence I gained in running helped me do better in school and in college. It gave me the courage to leave home and go to school somewhere else, which I could not have done without running.
>
> **–Kara Goucher**

You are a runner. You have initiative. Reflect for a moment on all the memories and life experiences, both good and bad, that running has given you. How many more days of your life do you remember because you are a runner? Think about all the ways you have displayed initiative through running. You have gotten off the couch and out the door; you have developed a vision of where you want to go as a runner and what it will take to get there. You have scheduled the time to get in your runs, do your push-ups and core work, and stretch. You know how to act and make things happen. You are the builder of your running life, the puppeteer in the story.

Children embody initiative and take action all the time. Think back to your childhood. Did you build forts? Create imaginary friends? Go on adventures with your real friends in the backyard? Did you explore and believe that anything was possible? Maybe you tried to cut your own hair or create a new recipe in the kitchen. Maybe you set out to draw a masterpiece with your crayons on the living room wall. No matter what your particular childhood was like, you had initiative. Many adults lose that admirable characteristic that children so effortlessly demonstrate. Adults stop acting and commence sitting. They trade a life of action for a life of reaction. The first attribute of the distance maven is simply how easy it is for us to get off the couch. This applies to both our running passion and our other four life stories.

WAY of the MAVEN

Mirror 1: Initiative

In each of the six chapters in Part 2, we will take a long look at some aspect of ourselves. We call this a mirror exercise. The goal of these chapters is to build a clear and comprehensive understanding of ourselves. We will take the thoughtful journey of personal enlightenment complimented by the lessons learned through running. Each mirror will reflect who we are right now and will show how much room we have for improvement. Be brutally honest with yourself in these mirror exercises. No one else needs to see your responses, so take a deep look at yourself and rate yourself as you are, not as you would like to be. (That comes in Part 3.)

Let's start with running. After you have decided on a goal and established a vision to get in shape or to run a particular race, the first thing you must do is get off the couch and act on that vision and desire. The way of distance mavens is the same. The ability to act, the wherewithal to get off the couch and do something, is vital to any attempt at self-improvement and life improvement. You can use what you know about yourself through running to help yourself take the initiative in your other life stories. If you cannot bring yourself to get off the couch at least sometimes, you will never achieve your running goals.

Honestly reflect on your initiative. Are you close to your ideal? Does your desire to run translate into getting yourself out the front door? Or do you sometimes lack sufficient drive to do your scheduled runs? Draw a ruler like the one pictured here, and on the line between the Reactor and the Distance Maven, place an *X* where you believe your running initiative lies.

Most likely, your initiative lies somewhere in the middle of this line, with room for improvement. No runner is perfect. We are all in progress. Acknowledging and becoming aware of who you are at this moment allows you to improve and measure your progress.

Now reflect on each of your life stories one at a time, and determine your level of initiative in each. Are you achieving all that you desire in your education, career, family, friendships, and other passions besides running? Do you recognize what needs to be changed or improved and then act on it? Is your success in each of your life stories limited to some degree by lack of action? Go back to your lists from Part 1. Look at the attributes you desire and the life stories you would like to improve. Now rate your level of initiative in each of your life stories. Remember to be honest, as it does no good to overestimate or deny areas where you could improve. Draw another ruler like the first one and mark a place on the line representing your initiative in your education, and label it with an *E*. Do the same for each life story, labeling your career with a *C*, family with an *F*, friendships with an *FR*, and passions with a *P*. Note: Do not include running in your passions, as it is ranked separately. Instead, think of your other personal interests, like golf, the piano, church groups, birding, and playing games.

You have taken the first strides in becoming a distance maven. You are now more aware of your level of initiative in your education, career, family, friendships, and passions. You can probably already see many ways to improve your initiative and in turn to improve your life stories, but take this assessment at face value for right now until you look in the other five mirrors. Each mirror will reveal another attribute and how it is affecting your running and life stories. When you have looked in all six mirrors, you will have an in-depth understanding of who you are and who you can become.

CHAPTER 7

There Is No One Else

RESPONSIBILITY

It is easy to dodge our responsibilities, but we cannot
dodge the consequences of dodging our responsibilities.
—Josiah Charles Stamp

If there is one lesson runners learn well, it is the connection between
their behavior and the consequences. By its very nature, running requires a certain amount of self-discipline and personal accountability.
If a runner misses the majority of his or her runs, slacks off during
workouts, or ignores proper nutrition, performance suffers. Likewise,
when runners consistently work hard, eat right, and do the things
needed to stay healthy, they almost always find success.

At the starting line, it may not be apparent who has put in the
work and who has not, but as the race treads on, each runner is
judged step by step for his or her actions in the days, weeks, months,
and even years leading up to the race. There is nowhere to hide from
this judgment, no one to blame or credit for what is happening. By

> It is important to not ever get so hard headed and dead set on doing something that you lose track of the big picture. One race or one workout is not worth setting yourself back several days or several weeks.
>
> **—Galen Rupp**

toeing the line, the runner has submitted to this sometimes cruel but always honest evaluation. Time is a cold-hearted arbiter of truth, and like it or not, a runner must take responsibility for the race and the results.

This is not to say that at times circumstances beyond a runner's control do not affect a race. Injury and illness often wreak havoc on even the most disciplined runner. In the cruelest twists of running fate, these factors seem far less fair than simple cause and effect. It is easier to accept harsh judgment when it is deserved, when we have not demonstrated the will to prepare. We can accept this blame and legitimate appraisal of our ability. But when we know we are ready for more and are dealt a losing hand anyway, we are alone, with no one else to bail us out.

THE LINE BETWEEN TOUGH AND STUPID

Adam

There is a fine line between tough and stupid. It is a line I have had trouble walking my whole life, and it has occasionally come back to haunt me. In 2000, I was the proud owner of my first home. It was a new home that needed a lot of work to finish. I could have hired a landscaper to finish the backyard, and a builder to put in a deck, but I thought it would be a fun challenge to do both myself. So one day, some of my good friends helped me work the auger as we drilled holes for the pilings of the deck. They helped dig the trenches for the new sprinkler system and haul eleven tons of gravel from the driveway to the backyard one wheelbarrow at a time.

The Olympic Trials were seven weeks away. The smart thing would have been to take it easy and rely on my friends to do the heavier lifting. I could have taken smaller loads in my wheelbarrow or just spread the work out over several days. But I had to be tough and outwork everyone else. That day, I was on the wrong side of the line between tough and stupid. Only several years later did I learn that on that day, I had suffered a bilateral sports hernia. All I knew was that my back hurt. I was also rushing back from an Achilles tendon injury and was hammering ninety miles a week without much base. The day after the dirt hauling, I went on a twenty-mile run, and by the end of the run, the sacroiliac joint in my lower back was killing me. Not wanting to miss a day of training, I pushed through.

The next day, despite the pain, I started my run. I was now on the wrong side of tough and stupid for the third straight day. Four miles into the run, I had to stop. The pain in my back was so severe I had to walk back home. I could not bend over, dry myself off when I got out of the shower, or even brush my teeth without severe discomfort. At the advice of my doctors, I had no choice but to stop running and allow my body to heal.

I took my first steps running again ten days before the 5000-meter prelims at the Olympic Trials. I did some basic jogging and felt OK, but I had missed almost five straight weeks of training and my confidence was at an all-time low.

In my preliminary heat, I ran as fast as I could. I knew I needed to be in the top six to advance automatically to the finals, but I could barely manage fifth. That race was incredibly hard, and I was not even close to the top three. How was I supposed to make it into the top three of the finals to make the Olympic team when I could barely get out of my heat? In the hours before that final, I had plenty of time to think. I was so frustrated. To be this close to achieving a lifelong goal, and now I could easily miss it. No one else could run this race for me. I would toe the line and take my shot. I would offer myself up to the cruel judgment of the clock, my competitors, and the public. There was nowhere to hide. There was no one else.

When the gun went off, I placed myself on the inside lane but way back in the pack. Two laps in, I was in thirteenth position, already 30 meters behind fourth place. By the mile, I had slowly worked my way to the front of the chase pack, running comfortably in sixth or seventh position, but Bob Kennedy had opened up a nearly 50-meter lead. At 3000 meters, Kennedy's lead had been closed by Marc Davis, and the pair led the chase pack by less than 30 meters. I knew I had to be patient and could not afford an early move. I needed to wait for the race to come to me, but I could feel the stiffness creeping into my legs. I had to keep shaking doubts from my mind. With two laps to go, Nick Rogers had taken the lead, followed closely by Marc Davis. I was next to Kennedy, along with Brad Hauser and Matt Lane, rounding out a pack of six. Three of us would make the Olympic team in the next two laps. I watched Nick Rogers stretch out to a big lead with a lap to go. I wanted to respond, but my legs seemed to be ignoring my mind. Pain seared my quadriceps and chest. I was hanging on by a thread. In the final lap, I summoned every stride of every workout I had ever run to help me. I beckoned every weight I lifted in pursuit of this goal, every morning I dragged my weary body out of bed to get in my morning run, every party I skipped, every choice I made in the last four years to help me in this moment. All that training had to be somewhere inside me. A few weeks off could not erase the previous four years! All those workouts had to be somewhere in the deep recesses of my capillaries, ready to lend what they could to the final surge.

Nick Rogers had a four-second gap on Brad Hauser and me, and it looked as though the race was for second. With 200 meters to go, I knew I had made the team, but something in me would not stop or settle for just making it. I needed to prove to myself that I belonged, and nothing less than the national championship would be good enough. My consciousness was sucked inside my body, where it wrapped itself up in muscle, blood, tendon, and bone. Everything looked as if it were shrouded in a red and black veil before I suddenly shot out of my body and watched myself from above the stadium as Brad Hauser and I overtook Nick Rogers. I broke the tape first, and everything went silent. For a brief moment, there was no pain. I tried to raise my arms in victory, but could not get them to rise past my shoulders. I was mercilessly slammed back into my body to deal with the agonizing pain of what I had done. I had never hurt that bad before or have since. It was as if my lungs were full of boiling oil, burning me from the inside out—the kind of pain that hurts days later just from the memory. But I had done it. There was no one else but me. I learned more about myself as a runner and a human being on that day than I had in any other single event in my life. I got closer to the edge of my potential than I had ever been and saw myself not for who I was but for who I could be.

> You are in charge of your own fate. You are the master of your own destiny. You can't blame a coach or anybody else. It is up to you to decide whose advice to take, but ultimately, you make the decision.
>
> **–Dathan Ritzenhein**

One of the first lessons running teaches us about success in athletics and in life is that there is no one else. No one else can do your workouts for you. You alone must do the drills, repeat the core exercises, stretch, and lift the weights. You cannot hire someone else to do your cross-training when you are battling injury, or pay someone to run a race and get you a new PR. You are truly your own hero in running. It is up to you to have the responsibility and self-discipline to get the job done. The way of the maven lies in how well you apply these lessons not only to running, but to your other life stories as well. In life, just like in running, there is no one else.

WAY OF THE REACTOR

What would a reactor do? Someone on the far left of the distance-maven gauge would be unaware of how a lack of responsibility, self-discipline, accountability, and reliability affects success in running and in life. Let's consider an extreme example of a fictional character named Mr. O'Tool. Mr. O'Tool has dreams of being a great runner (passion), a successful businessman (career), and a caring husband and father (family). But his dreams remain dreams because he lacks the discipline to follow through. His grand plans of training sixty miles a week are continually foiled as he keeps postponing his workouts until tomorrow, when the weather will be better and he will have had a better night's sleep, or his favorite movie isn't playing on TV. Every time he does manage to get in a run, he is shocked to see how little progress he has made.

Mr. O'Tool's lack of responsibility influences his other life stories as well. At the beginning of each month, he spends his paycheck on magazines, restaurants, electronics, and new clothes, then wonders why he cannot pay his rent or make his car payment. He forgets to set his alarm clock, shows up late to work, and gets bad reviews. He borrows things from his friends and never returns them and wonders why they stop taking his calls.

What's even worse than the problems brought on by his irresponsibility, Mr. O'Tool views all these problems as not his fault. His job needs to pay him more for his work, so the money won't run out. His boss is unreasonable and should forgive the occasional sleep-in day. His friends didn't need the things he borrowed as much as he did, so why should he return them? With Mr. O'Tool, there is always an excuse and always someone else to blame.

Even his lack of discipline in running is not his fault. The weather is too hot or too cold. His shoes are still wet from the day before. He missed lunch, because his boss made him work to make up for being late. When he has a bad race, it is because the bathroom line was too long and he did not get to go, or because his shoelaces came untied, or because . . . Mr. O'Tool is a reactor, nothing more than a tool of circumstance, unable to create a better situation. When looking for the cause of his failure, Mr. O'Tool will look everywhere except in the mirror, and when he needs someone to blame, he will point his finger everywhere but at himself.

RESPONSIBILITY IS NO JOKE

Legend has it that about fifty years ago, a man was worried that his wife might be losing her hearing. Knowing she would be very self-conscious about it, he went to visit their family doctor to see what he could do. The doctor told the man to go back home and do a simple test to see the extent of her hearing loss. He said to stand behind her and ask her a question from twenty feet away, then from ten feet away, and finally from five feet away. This would give the husband an idea of how bad her hearing loss had become. So the man goes home and finds his wife facing the stove, cooking something. He asks her from twenty feet away, "What's for dinner tonight?" No response. He moves forward, now only ten feet away, and asks the same question. Still no response. Finally, he is standing right behind her and asks again, "What's for dinner tonight?" She turns around and says to him, "For the third time, I am telling you it's chicken!"

It is much easier to look at other people or situations as the cause of a problem. It is more difficult to look at ourselves. Further, if the problem is with other people or situations, then the solution to that problem is largely out of our control. If we look to ourselves first and see what we are contributing to an issue, we are empowered to change the situation by changing ourselves and how we are affecting the problem.

It was autumn and winter was quickly approaching. On a reservation, a nervous new chief of a Native American tribe was asked by his people if it was going to be a cold winter. The chief did not know, as he had not bothered to learn the old, reliable methods of predicting the weather. Just to be safe, he told his people it would be a cold winter and instructed them to start gathering wood. A few weeks later, he decided to call the National Weather Service just to be sure. When he asked the staff member if it was going to be a cold winter, the person told him it looked as though it would be pretty cold. Confident, the chief went back to his people and ordered them to gather even more wood. A week later, he called the National Weather Service people again to see if the forecast had changed. They told him that it indeed looked like an even colder winter than they had originally thought. So the chief went back to his people and asked them to collect every scrap of wood they could find, because they probably would need it all. A few weeks later, the chief checked in with the Weather Service one last time. This time, they told him it might be one of the coldest winters on record. "How can you be so sure?" asked the chief. The Weather Service replied, "The Native Americans are gathering wood like crazy!"

When we fail to do the work and take responsibility for ourselves, we are living a lie. We are taking credit for work that is not our own, or we are laying blame where it does not belong. We must have the accountability to do it ourselves, the self-discipline to follow through, and the awareness that we are responsible for making our own success. In the absurd story above, the National Weather Service was relying on someone else to do the work it should have been doing itself. Likewise, the chief was not accountable to his people, as he never learned to predict the weather. Without the final question of "How can you be so sure?" which illustrates the faulty reasoning used by both, the predictions may or may not have been accurate. What's more, neither party would have understood the reason for the failure and most likely would have blamed the other party for the lapse. Like most people, the chief and the National Weather Service staff would have been left unaware of the part they had played in their own lack of success. Both parties in this story needed to look in the mirror.

As runners, we are all fortunate in that we learn to have a great sense of personal responsibility in our running. We know that we are the only ones who can do the work necessary to make ourselves better runners. Our self-discipline, reliability, and conscientiousness all feed our ability to train and do the myriad other little things needed to run at the levels we expect of ourselves. We realize that there is no one else. We are not afraid to look in the mirror and see the reflection of our choices and actions and, when necessary, point the finger of blame squarely at our own chest.

The way of the distance maven is to become aware of these lessons, to look deep within ourselves and to examine our levels of responsibility, and then to make conscious choices about how to improve. When we understand that we have what it takes to be responsible in our running, we can apply that self-knowledge to our other life stories as well. In this way, we can live up to our pledge of excellence in everything.

But how do we maintain this level of personal responsibility when the prevailing winds of inertia, fatigue, or adversity are blowing directly into our faces, encouraging us to stop? The next chapter describes just what a distance maven needs to face these situations.

Mirror 2: Responsibility

The task for this chapter is to assess your level of responsibility with the help of the self-evaluations you have made thus far. First, recall the list of difficult things you have accomplished thus far in running (from Chapter 4). Keeping in mind these accomplishments and the distance-maven characteristics you have and you want to have (from Chapters 3 and 5), assess your responsibility and discipline in accomplishing your goals in running. On a scale like the one pictured, mark this estimated level of responsibility between the reactor and the distance maven.

This mark represents your responsibility in running—the level of success you have had in getting as close to your edge as possible. You can, of course, use this exercise to work on improving your level of responsibility in running, but you can also use it to compare your levels of responsibility in your other life stories with your level in running.

To make this comparison, on a second, similar scale, place a vertical dash on the line representing your assessment of your responsibility in each of your five life stories. Mark each dash, as appropriate, with *E* for education, *C* for career, *F* for family, *FR* for friendship, or *P* for passions. Remember, the more honestly and closely you examine your reflection, the more power you will have in creating the life you want to live.

Is your responsibility in running higher than it is in your other life stories? Can you imagine how much better your other life stories would be if you raised your level of responsibility in these aspects of your life?

CHAPTER 8

Then Comes the Hill

DETERMINATION

Tim

My dad asked my mom to marry him six times. She refused five of those times.

They met in college at a community square dance. They bowed to each other, did a do-si-do, swung each other round and round, and fell in love. My mom was hesitant to get involved with a small-town Catholic boy, but my dad was convinced he had just met the girl of his dreams. He came home after that first date and told his roommates that he had met the girl he was going to marry. They laughed and joked with him, but he knew for sure that this was the real thing.

My mom remembers him asking her out every weekend, and despite her resistance, she was finding him irresistible. Her parents were not in favor of the new Catholic boy, and my mom knew she did not want to raise children in a home where the parents go to different churches. So to get away from him and the confusion, she signed a contract for a teaching position in Michigan for the following year. She would move away and avoid further heartbreak. My dad had to act fast, so only two months after that first dance, he proposed for the first time.

He was willing to become a Methodist and raise their children under one church, and he saw no other reason they should not be together. But the teaching contract was already signed. She would be leaving in a few months and had to say no. She broke his heart. Fortunately, it was a resilient heart, and by the next weekend, they were on another date. He asked again. The second no was easier to take, as he had already been rejected and knew how it felt. He was not afraid.

This pattern went on for several more weeks. He would ask her as if it were the first time, and she would list all the logical reasons it would never work. Finally, on a long weekend, he asked her to meet his family and spend the weekend in the little town where he had grown up. She agreed, believing she had the strength to resist his persistent proposals. The logical side of her mind knew it would not work, but her emotions were screaming for a different answer. Although she had agreed to go home with him for the weekend, she was nervous that she would not be able to resist much longer. My dad and my grandmother conspired in the kitchen as Grandma helped him pack a picnic lunch for the two young people to take to the mountains. He borrowed Grandma's ruby ring to use as a prop in his next proposal attempt. He wanted his girl-friend to feel a ring on her finger and imagine their lives together. Logic be damned. They were meant to be together.

He waited for the right moment after they had settled down on their blanket to enjoy the blue sky and fresh mountain air. He slipped the ruby ring on her finger and asked again. She gazed at the ring, looked at my dad, and said, "Now that you have put it on me, you are not allowed to take it off!" They would have to spend the first year of their engagement apart, while she honored her contract, but she believed they both had the determination to make it work. Forty-four years later, they are still making it work.

Good thing my dad was a distance runner!

Determination, tenacity, commitment, and perseverance are the hall-marks of the distance runner. Show us a distance runner who gives up easily or does not stick it out through the rough patches, and we will show you a very poor runner. Running re-quires levels of determination and persevere-ance unparalleled in other sports. The urge to throw in the towel and concede defeat constantly nags at a runner during races, dur-ing workouts, and even between runs. But as George Sheehan so aptly describes in his book *Running and Being*, through our sport we discover that we are made for more. Be-cause we choose to endure pain, and bear hardship, we are able to reach the very limits of our physiology. Because we are not afraid to choose suffering we discover the end of what is possible. Sheehan writes,

> When we first got our place in France, we started to cross-country ski, but I could not turn left. I went around and around in circles until I got it right.
>
> **–Paula Radcliffe**

> . . . [G]radually the hill demands more and more . . . it is beyond what I can stand. The temptation is to say, "Enough." This much is enough. But I will not give in. I am fighting God. Fighting the limitations He gave me. Fighting the pain. Fighting the unfairness. Fighting all the evil in me and in the world. And I will not give in. I will conquer this hill, and I will conquer it alone.

Midrace, when it really starts to hurt and there is still a lot of suf-fering to be done before the finish line signals the end of our self-inflicted abuse, we are faced with several choices: We can stop and walk (not an option), we can slow down and give up a few places or pre-cious seconds (not an option), we can maintain our pace and accept that it is going to hurt for a while longer (a good option), or we can drop the hammer, speed up, and see how much more pain we can take (great option!). The same choices face us during workouts, long runs, and even easy days. Runners learn that if they just keep going, they will reach the finish line and a well-earned rest before the next battle. They will feel better about their accomplishments and themselves because they persevered instead of giving up.

Most of us have experimented with the easy path at one time or another. On occasion, most runners dabble with giving up, thinking it won't be that bad, but in the end, their own conscience gets to them and makes them promise not to let themselves down again. We cannot think of a context, outside of running, that allows people to practice determination at the same level. On a daily basis, we get to reveal our level of commitment and our willingness to pay the price.

ROCK BOTTOM

Adam

The 2004 Olympic Trials could not have been more different for me than what happened in 2000. I had battled an endless string of injuries since I had made that first Olympic team. My doctors and others were concerned that I had damaged myself to the point I might never get back. Still, I toed the line again with dreams of pulling off another upset and making another Olympic team.

In my preliminary heat, I finished tenth out of twelve runners. Later, I could not even bring myself to watch Tim Broe claim the national title and Olympic berth I had held four years earlier. Doubts and other negative thoughts dominated my mind. For the first time in my life, I had given up before the race even started. I was so frustrated because I did not even recognize who I was. This did not feel like me. I had finally completed my journey to rock bottom. "This is as bad as it gets," I thought. I was wrong.

I looked to my coach, Mark Wetmore, for some solace and support, but he had also reached rock bottom with me.

"You might have to accept that this is as good as it gets," he said.

His words were like salt in my open wounds. He was trying to comfort me, but I was not comforted. I was enraged.

He continued, "You have been through a lot and achieved many re-markable things, but those days might be behind you."

Confusion flooded my mind. Was he telling me to retire? Was he telling me that he no longer believed in me? Was he right? Did I even be-lieve in myself?

I felt empty, lost, confused. All I knew at that point was running. Run-ning carried me to where I was in life. It was my identity, and it was about to be taken away. To make matters worse, my wife, Kara, was going through similar trials. With her career also on the downside, we both had to face the hard reality that maybe our best days were behind us. Maybe it was time to move on. We bought some books to help us make the tran-sition into lives after professional running.

Kara called her best friend, Anna, for some advice and had a con-versation that changed everything for both of us.

"Do you think I should quit?" Kara asked.

"Well, do you want to be done? How does it make you feel to think about stopping running?"

"It makes me sad," Kara said without hesitation.

"Well then, there is your answer!" With those words, Kara gained some clarity not so much on the status of her remaining ability, but on the status of her heart and desire.

That night, when Kara asked me the same question, I had the same answer. We were united in our belief that we were not done. At that point, we realized that we had two choices. We could hang it up and walk away, or we could make some changes, start over, and lead with our hearts. It was an invigorating feeling that scared the hell out of both of us.

The point of no return came as Kara and I sat in Mark's office hav-ing one of the most difficult conversations of our lives. It was like a hor-rible breakup. To this day, there are few men who I admire or respect more than Mark Wetmore. I am thankful for everything he did for me, how he taught me, and how he trained me. The thought of leaving him was excruciating, but it had to be done. There were hurt feelings, tears, and several painful moments as we agreed to go our separate ways, but the moment we walked out of his office, our depression turned to optimism and the road ahead. We would start from scratch and rebuild ourselves from the ground up.

Nike put us in touch with Alberto Salazar, who immediately won us over with his optimism that he could help us get headed back in the right direction. He had never coached a woman before, but liked what he saw in Kara and wanted to give it a try. He believed in us perhaps more than we believed in ourselves at that point, and it was exactly what we needed.

Like something out of a *Rocky* movie, Kara and I attacked our comebacks with relentless energy. Our morning workouts alone could last five hours by the time we ran, lifted, did our core exercises and drills, and stretched. Then it was home for lunch and a nap before the afternoon session. Every waking moment was occupied with bringing our bodies, minds, and fitness back to elite levels. We had never worked so hard, and we had never been as happy.

Seven months after hitting rock bottom at the Track and Field Olympic Trials, I finished second, only a meter back from Tim Broe, and qualified for the world cross-country team. A year later, I would win that national title and go on to finish sixth at the World Cross Country Championships, only eight seconds off the win. I was back on top, and even if it did not last, I had proven to myself how important it is to persevere through the hard times, to cling to my dreams with stubborn persistence, and to let my heart lead the way. Kara's story followed a similar path and resurgence. She continues to be my biggest source of inspiration, support, friendship, and love.

Not all of us have running stories that include Olympic trials and world championship races. Most of us fight our running battles in community 10K runs, in marathons, or just in our daily workouts. But the lessons are the same. The Olympian does not necessarily possess greater determination than the weekend road warrior who fights back from injury, burnout, or other setbacks. It is not the level of achievement or the numbers attached to a PR that are important. It is the size of our hearts. It is what we do in those moments when all hope seems lost and we are confronted with a choice to give up or keep trying. It is what we learn about ourselves through those dire circumstances that gives us the courage and strength to conquer the other challenges and hills in our lives.

In each of our five life stories, determination plays an important role. If we can apply the same levels of determination we exhibit in running to our educations, careers, families, friendships, and other passions, then we are more likely to reach the levels of success we imagined in the most optimistic days of our youth.

Reflect again on the lists of accomplishments you made at the end of Chapter 4. You have chosen to do many difficult things in your life. Reflect on how much courage, determination, and tenacity it took to accomplish each of those things. These qualities are evidence that you are not just a reactor. They show that you have what it takes to see things through—that you have the backbone and guts to follow your heart.

After not making the Olympic team in 2008, I had thoughts of "Why am I doing this?" It was a devastating blow, and I needed to re-evaluate myself: where I was at with my running and where I was at with my life. Later on, because I had questioned myself, I came back with more piss and vinegar.

Every 5K I ran last year [Chris ran under 13 minutes three times], there was a point in the race where I contemplated dropping out because of how bad I was hurting or doubting myself. But I just kept hanging on for one more lap to see if I could get through it. Earlier in my career, I did give up in a few races, and I would be so angry at myself and I didn't want it to happen again.

–Chris Solinsky

WHAT WOULD A REACTOR DO?

In the last chapter, we met a character named Mr. O'Tool, an example of a person with an utter lack of responsibility. This time, let's say that Mr. O'Tool has a wife who is equally a victim of circumstance and unable to take charge to build the life she wants to live. What Mr. O'Tool lacks in responsibility, Mrs. O'Tool matches in her tendency to give up at the first sign of difficulty. Mrs. O'Tool lives by the mottos "When the going gets tough, give up," and "If at first you don't succeed, stop trying."

She tried running several times, but stopped after developing a blister or accidentally getting her heart rate over 140 beats per minute. In her first race, she dropped out halfway through because she felt a cramp coming. Her lack of determination displayed in her running also showed up in her other life stories. In school, when she did not get a concept right away, she threw her hands up in defeat and declared, "This is too hard!" In her career, she might have climbed the ladder for a promotion, but she could not figure out how to attach her résumé to the application, so she never sent it. When she and Mr. O'Tool had difficulties in their relationship, she refused to face the tough issues or to put in the work necessary to make it work. Likewise with her daughter, Mrs. O'Tool lacked the courage to set rules and standards and to stick to them. Even her friendships suffered from Mrs. O'Tool's lack of determination. She just could not make herself stick by her friends in the rough times or work hard to make the relationships last. Poor Mrs. O'Tool. How much better a life she could have created for herself if she had just learned to be determined, persistent, and courageous enough to stick to her commitments.

> I have given up in races. You get to a point when it is all falling apart. Those are the worst days, because not only do you fail in a race, but you have to go home knowing you quit.
>
> **–Kara Goucher**

From their experience in running, distance mavens learn that they have what it takes to see things through. Running isn't easy, and neither is life. A marriage will fall on hard times. Friendships will experience difficult patches. Careers require high levels of perseverance, and education is most effective when students struggle with new learning before developing mastery.

The same determination and tenacity that turn ordinary humans into distance runners can help runners bring their ordinary lives closer to the edge. If we are to be true to the way of the distance maven, then we need to be honest with ourselves about the level of determination we have in running and in each of our life stories.

THE STARING CONTEST

Tim

In college, I once had a staring contest with a candle. It was just a little tea light burning on the windowsill behind the couch. I was about to blow it out and go to bed, when I noticed that it was flickering for life, just about to exhaust the last of its fuel resources and die on its own. It was interesting to watch, so instead of blowing it out, I decided to watch it complete its natural life span. As I watched it gasp, in what I believed were its final moments, I felt a contemplative peace in this simple act of watching this candle. Twenty minutes later, my contemplation turned to curiosity as to how this candle was still burning. It was well after midnight, and I had an eight o'clock class in the morning. I gave the candle ten more minutes before I allowed my peaceful contemplation to turn into utter contempt. It was just like when a friendly, easy six-mile run with a friend somehow turns into a race. Did this candle think it was tougher than me? Did it think it could outlast me or that I would give up and blow it out? I resolved in my mind that I could not allow this candle to beat me. It was just like Sheehan's hill, and I needed to conquer this challenge!

Adding to my irritation, I really needed to go to the bathroom. I had been drinking a lot of water while I watched a movie, and my bladder was at maximum capacity. The candle would not yield, and neither would I. I shifted positions to alleviate the pressure on my bladder and shook my head from side to side to ward off sleep. It was on. This was war.

My roommate came home about 1:30 A.M. to find me squirming on the couch. I greeted him without looking away from my rival or explaining what

I was doing in an otherwise dark room, staring at a single light source. He sauntered off to bed, leaving me to finish this battle alone. I wished I would never have started this silly game, but I was in too deep to give up now. I had come too far and invested too much time to lose. I felt as if the universe were conspiring against me. I did not know how much longer I could fight off sleep or keep from wetting my pants.

I've suffered worse, I thought to myself as I conjured up visions of runs and races where I pushed through similar amounts of pain. *Bring it on, you worthless candle! You have no idea who you are dealing with!* My false bravado and internal pep talk bought me precious minutes, but I was running out of time. I had to stay focused, stay determined, stay committed.

Finally, just before 2:00 A.M., the candle gave up and died. I made a victory dash to the bathroom and allowed myself to savor the triumph as I relieved myself. It was a good fight with a worthy opponent. I crawled into my comfortable bed with a gratified smile, feeling as if there were not a problem in the world I could not solve.

The previous story sounds silly, and indeed it was a silly thing to do, but as we illustrated earlier, runners are a bit crazy. They love a challenge and do not wish to live normal lives. Maybe you don't get into staring contests with candles, but do you find other ways to test your limits, commitment, and determination? We're guessing that you do!

WAY of the MAVEN

Initiative
Pro-Activity
Vision
Optimism
Confidence
Resourcefulness

Responsibility
Reliability
Accountability
Conscientious
Sensible
Self Discipline

Determination
Perseverance
Courage
Tenacity
Focus
Commitment

Mirror 3: Determination

The technique is the same one we used in the last two chapters. First, take a look at your running, and honestly assess your level of determination on a scale from 1 to 10, or from reactor to distance maven. Do you sometimes give up when you could push through? In a hard workout or race, when you are certain that you have reached your pain limit, can you still hold on until the end? Do you have a sharp focus on what you want to accomplish and the courage to stick to that plan through the ups and downs that come with running? On a scale like the one pictured, mark your level of determination in running.

Next, go through each of your life stories one at a time, and take the same hard look in the mirror. Do you continue to push, struggle, and learn in your educational life story even when the learning is difficult, or do you give up and decide it is too hard? Do you work relentlessly to overcome obstacles in your career to achieve your dreams, or do you settle for what is comfortable, familiar, and easy? Do you work hard on your intimate relationships? What about your roles as a father or mother as well as a son or daughter? Do you work on all these family relationships when things are difficult, or do you give up or accept things as they are? Likewise with your friendships, do you put in the work necessary to make them work? Are you persistent in your efforts to be a good friend? Finally, in your other passions outside of running, are you determined to improve at them, perform at a high level, master new challenges, and keep going when you hit a plateau or valley? Now, draw a scale similar to the one you have done for running, and mark your estimated level of determination for each of these five life stories, labeling the lines with an *E* for education, a *C* for career, and so forth.

You now have a visual representation of your determination as it applies to running and each of your five life stories. This is another angle of awareness showing you who you are. If you have been honest in your assessments, then you now can clearly see how you embody determination and where there is room for improvement.

CHAPTER 9

When to Bend

ADAPTABILITY

Can runners have too much initiative, self-discipline, and determination? Can an overabundance of these attributes get in the way of their success? In some situations in life, we need to react to unforeseen circumstances, adapt our visions, or change our plans. If we are overly rigid, uncompromising, and unwilling to bend, those other positive attributes can work against us rather than for us. Adaptability brings balance to the first three attributes of the distance maven.

The difference between reactors and the adaptability of distance mavens is that mavens have a vision and have taken the initiative to set a plan in motion. Mavens take responsibility for building the lives they desire and are determined to follow through with their plans. Reactors never get this far. But there are times in every life story where plans must change and schedules must be altered. Initiative, responsibility, and determination must be tempered by adaptability.

> I am not good at taking time off for injury so sometimes I have too much motivation.
>
> **—Paula Radcliffe**

HOW TO RUIN EVERYTHING

Let's create one more character, Junior O'Tool. Imagine that Junior had just graduated from college and was on a fast track to success in all five of his life stories. He had earned a business degree, had been offered a job in a successful company, was recently married, had a small group of close friends, and was an avid runner training for his first marathon. His education, career, family, friendships, and passions all seemed primed for success. Even with so many aspects of his life in alignment, if he were too rigid and did not know when to bend, he could have jeopardized all of his potential.

With his degree in hand, Junior O'Tool considered himself educated. Why would he need to continue learning about evolving business practices, market conditions, and technology when he was already certified with that magical piece of paper? In his job, Junior did things strictly by the book. Too bad his book was already ten years old. He had learned a set of skills and strategies and used them exclusively. As competitive companies began to adapt their marketing strategies to incorporate new technologies, Junior O'Tool refused to change his ways. "Facebook?" exclaimed Junior. "We were doing just fine without Facebook before, so why would we need it now?"

In his marriage, Junior O'Tool was equally uncompromising. The plan was for him to work and for his wife to stay home and start having children. As Junior continued to be passed over for promotion after promotion, the couple's financial situation became unstable. His wife

> I was scheduled to race a 5k one week prior to the Olympic Trials, but I had to drop out halfway through because my calf was very sore. It was very disappointing to drop out of a race, but it was the right decision and it kept my leg from getting worse. The next week we took things very easy and I kept my focus on controlling the things I could control so I could make the team. I ended up getting 2nd in the 10,000 meters and fulfilling my dream of becoming an Olympian. To this day it remains one of my proudest moments.
>
> **–Galen Rupp**

was offered a job earning three times his salary, but Junior would not have it. That was not the plan; it would require a move to a new town and a new job for him. No. They would follow their original plan.

As his college friends got jobs, moved farther away, and began their families, Junior could not understand why the poker tournaments and boys' nights out gave way to potlucks, birthday parties, and family picnics. He missed how life was "back in the day," and he refused to adapt to his friends' changing lives. Over time, most of his friendships disappeared.

With his running, Junior was following to the letter a marathon plan he had found in a running magazine. When his knee became sore, he ran anyway. When a family reunion or another event would require him to move a long run to a different day, he stubbornly refused to change his schedule and would instead miss the event. A mild flu bug grabbed hold of him six weeks before a race. Two days of rest would have put him back to full strength, but he refused to modify his training. As a result, the symptoms got worse and lasted several weeks. He was not physically ready to run the time he had set as a goal, but he went out on those splits anyway, refusing to change his plan. When the marathon turned into a disaster, Junior hung up his running shoes for good.

The problem with Junior O'Tool was that he did not know *when to bend* and when to stand firm. He lacked the critical attribute of *adaptability*. He was stubborn, uncompromising, closed-minded, and unable to change with shifting circumstances. In most aspects of his life, he confused commitment and determination with accommodation and compromise. In our running, we must be able to adapt. Our determination and tenacity must be tempered by an open mind and a willingness to change. As distance mavens, our nature is to be proactive and to create our own set of circumstances, but we must also be able to react when forces beyond our control require a change. An unexpected injury does not have to be the end of the world. Maybe we can cross-train on a bike or in the pool. An illness might require that we take a few days off to recover quickly. In a race, we need to be able to match an opponent's unexpected moves or adapt to weather conditions or to an unexpectedly slow or fast pace. Adaptability is critical to success in running and in life.

CHANGING OF THE GUARD

Adam

It was 1999, and I was entering my first outdoor track season as a professional runner. I was coming off national championships in both cross-country and indoor track, but I had yet to measure myself against the reigning king of American distance running, Bob Kennedy. The man had numerous national championships and American records to his credit. He was, at the time, the only American to run under 13:00 in the 5K. Nike made two styles of racing shoes with his name on them. He was deservedly the face of American distance running, and I wanted a shot at him. Internally, I was in awe of Bob Kennedy, but I would never let it show on the outside.

At a meet in Long Island, a few weeks before the national championships, I got my first chance as a professional athlete to race this legend. It was a 3000-meter race stacked with talent from Africa and the United States. I was eager to mix it up with this quality competition and vowed not to be intimidated.

I sat back in the lead pack as the race unfolded and waited for some of the early pretenders to drop off. With three laps to go, I made sure I was in position and waited to make my move. In front of me were two Africans and Kennedy. I surged to the lead with 350 meters to go in the final lap. I was laying all my cards on the table and calling all bluffs. I could taste the finish line less than fifty seconds away.

Coming off the final curve, one of the African runners moved past my right shoulder. I bore down, searching for one last gear to get me to the line. When another African runner started to pass, I tried even harder. Then, with only 15 meters to go, I saw him. The runner every American runner feared, not yet ready to hand me his crown. He lunged past me for third place while I had to settle for fourth. I was disappointed in the loss, but Kennedy no longer seemed unbeatable. Still, I knew I would need to adapt and change my strategy if I wanted a different outcome the next time we raced.

I watched the film of that race over and over again to see how it played out. I noticed that my form changed over the final 60 meters as my extra effort actually slowed me down, causing me to overstride. I knew I needed to correct this problem as well as adapt my race plan if I wanted to beat Kennedy in two weeks at nationals.

During those two weeks, I practiced sprinting while tired, purposely chopping my stride and trying to keep my body leaning in front of my legs. I also developed a plan I hoped would catch Kennedy off guard and allow me to take the 5000-meter crown from him.

Six laps into the race at nationals, Kennedy made his move. I had seen it on film many times before: He would throw down a couple blazing laps to create a gap, breaking the collective will of the field. I was ready for this move and committed to matching it. I saw him glance over his shoulder to see if anyone had gone with him. He did a double take as if surprised to see me. I thought, *That's right. I am still here.* He then slowed, almost forcing me to take the lead. I darted to the front and thought to myself, *He thinks he will just kick me down in the final stretch, like he did in the 3K.* I had to be ready.

I continued to lead heading into the final lap, but I could feel him on my shoulder. I watched him out of my peripheral vision with 250 meters to go. I knew he wanted to surprise me with a big move, but I would surprise him instead. As soon as he flinched to make his move, I exploded into my finishing kick. No more overstriding. No clumsy gait to the finish. I was relaxed, fluid, and in control. The elation of winning that race was greater than any other race up to that point in my career. I felt as if I had finally arrived. I knocked off the king of American running. In my mind, it was the changing of the guard. But this would not be my last battle with Bob Kennedy.

In 2001, it was his turn to adapt. If he wanted to beat me, he would have to bend and alter his own style. He knew how I liked to race and how I always looked to match moves. This time, he would use it against me. In that race, I was ready to run a fast pace if that was how it unfolded. Confident in my speed, I was also ready to lay back and win in a kickers' duel. But I was not ready for what Kennedy did.

He altered his pace on almost every lap. He surged and slowed down. Predictably, I matched his moves, letting him dictate my race. I had not trained for this. The constant changing of speeds slowly sapped my strength and drained my kick. In the final stretch, I had nothing left. I was outmatched by a clever champion that day—a champion who knew how to adapt to changing conditions and competitors. He taught me yet another lesson that day and reclaimed his crown.

Many runners struggle with adaptability. They have learned the connection between hard work and success and have developed a strong sense of dedication and determination to continue pushing their limits. They demonstrate daily that they are not reactors as they shape themselves into better athletes mile after mile. They continuously take action day after day, but to reach their maximum potential, they must also learn to adapt to changing circumstances. They must alter plans to deal with unexpected weather or aches and pains. They need to compromise with their training partners to find agreeable workout days. During a race, they must pay attention not only to their competitors but also to their own internal data. A planned 400-meter finishing sprint can stretch to 600 or shrink to 200, depending on how they are feeling or how much energy they had to spend in the middle to maintain pace. Show us a runner who is unwilling to adapt, and we will show you a runner who won't last very long.

WALKING THE LINE

In Chapter 7, we discussed the fine line between tough and stupid. In running and life, there are times when we need to be tough, refuse to give in, cling to our vision, and fight through obstacles standing in our way. At other times, we need to know when to bend. We need to be willing to adapt to unpredictable circumstances before our own tenacity pushes us across to the stupid side of the line. We must find a balance between determination and adaptability.

When to bend is not a science or an equation you can calculate. It is a judgment call based on available data. Adam's story about landscaping his yard before the Olympic Trials is a good example of not knowing when to bend. He ended up on the wrong side of the line. Not wanting to be a reactor, he was unwilling to recognize the wisdom in altering his actions. Likewise, Tim's story about running Bear Peak is another good example of how to make the wrong decision by having too much determination and too little adaptability when walking the line.

> I have been very selfish with my time and all the time I need to spend training and recovering. Now that I am married, I have adapted my lifestyle to be more accommodating to another person's schedule.
>
> **–Chris Solinsky**

On the other hand, we can also be too flexible. We can end up taking unnecessary days off in our running when we should have pushed through. We run the risk of compromising too much. Knowing when to bend also means knowing when to stand firm.

NAKED DEATH QUEST

Tim

We thought spring had finally arrived in Colorado with the warmer days and more comfortable running conditions welcomed by a team tired of running in ski hats and sweatshirts. We had just enjoyed our first track meet of the year under bright blue skies. Some of the kids were even sporting sunburns. But winter was not willing to go away without delivering one last punch.

It was Monday, and I had scheduled a workout we lovingly referred to as *Death Quest*, but probably more commonly known as *Point of Reference*. In this workout, runners do loops around a 500-meter grass circuit full of hills and sharp turns. They run for three minutes before the whistle blows, signaling them to stop. As soon as they hear the whistle, the runners look for a point of reference. It could be a rock, a tree, a picnic table, or one of the many cones outlining the course. They get two and a half minutes to recover and make their way back to the starting line for the next repetition. The object of the workout is to go a little farther past the point of reference in each of these three-minute intervals. Depending on the runner, the workout includes somewhere between three and six repetitions.

The runners always loved it when I explained the name *Death Quest* to the newcomers. "The object of this workout," I began, "is to run so hard that your heart explodes and you die!" This always got their attention. "No one has ever run that hard, but today you are going to try. If you can run so hard that your heart actually explodes, you will become an instant legend! You will always be known as 'that guy' or 'that girl' who ran so hard their heart exploded! In honor of your effort, we will name the track after you, and your name will live on as a testament to your courage!" For some reason, this morbid pre-workout speech worked well on teenagers. They attacked this workout as if they had every intention of becoming a legend.

But on this particular day in early spring, Mother Nature threw a twist into our plans of achieving ultimate running glory in our quest for death. A light mist and an icy wind had combined to encase each blade of newly green grass in ice. The field was slick, the temperature was below freezing, and the wind chill made the dull gray sky even more ominous. The sprinters, throwers, hurdlers, and jumpers all had their practices moved to the weight room, and their workouts postponed until the following day. The distance team was not so lucky.

We met in the hallway just outside the gym. All thirty-five distance runners were wearing their baggy school-issued gray sweatpants and tops, with multiple layers underneath. They sat in a semicircle looking up at me with pleading eyes. I knew what was on their minds. They wanted me to postpone Death Quest until tomorrow or even next week. They wanted to do anything other than go outside, but were afraid I would stick to the plan, unwilling to bend. I contemplated the risks. I knew the course was slick, but I also knew that since the course was on grass, a fall would not hurt them. Moreover, although it was cold, the warm hallways of the school were only 300 meters away. I was walking the line between tough and stupid and contemplating if it was time to bend.

I cleared my throat and the team fell silent. "There comes a time in every season," I paused deliberately to allow the anticipation to build, "when we have to look at the weather outside with sheer defiance and utter insubordination. On that day, we must look outside and proclaim, 'You are not tougher than me!'" I could see the disappointment on their faces, but I continued with an intentionally overdramatic tone, "Today is that day! Today we will prove to ourselves, and to Mother Nature, that we are made for more. We will not submit to her will, or give in to our own impulses to take the easy road. Today is a day made for Death Quest. Today is a good day to die!" Some of their eyes lit up as they began to smell a fun challenge, wanting to test their limits. The other half of the team needed more convincing.

"The normal parameters still stand. Group One will do a minimum of three repetitions, Group Two will do four, Group Three will do five, and the top group should do all six." The standing rules of Death Quest were that every runner had a minimum, but was free to challenge himself or herself to do more. If the runner was scheduled for three but wanted to do an extra one, I would always say yes. I expected only about seven runners to do all six.

I was not done: "I don't know about you, but I am furious at the weather today for thinking it can change our plans! Doesn't Mother Nature know who we are?" The runners looked at me, apparently wondering where I was going with this. "I have a proposal for all of you monsters who want to defy Mother Nature in the ultimate act of contempt,

disregard, and insolence. Any runner who completes the first five repetitions and chooses to do a sixth, I will let strip down and do it 'naked.'"
Now I had their full attention. "Not completely naked, but down to the clothes you would wear on the hottest day in the summer to go for a run. It will be the classic humans-versus-nature story, and we will be victorious!" The energy level suddenly spiked as their minds processed the challenge. Suddenly, this viciously cold day full of potential misery became an adventure, and they were up for the challenge.

It was the only time in my five years coaching at Eaglecrest High School where every last runner chose to do all six intervals in Death Quest. Just before the last one, thirty-five runners stripped down to their split shorts and threw off their gloves and hats. The guys went shirtless, the girls in either sport bras or T-shirts. Just before I gave the signal to begin, the team let out a primal scream of defiance right in the face of Mother Nature.

The windows of the school building were lined with spectators staring in disbelief as these runners ran for all they were worth around the icy field wearing as little clothing as allowed by law. High fives, hugs, and more screams followed the team on the brief "cool-down" before the kids went back inside to stretch and reminisce about one of the most memorable workouts of their lives. No one died that day, but they all became legends.

Knowing when to bend is an art form, not a science. We cannot always be flexible and accommodating, or we risk compromising our way right out of achieving our goals. When we find ourselves walking that line between tough and stupid, we have to stop and ask an important and honest question: Is it time to bend or time to stand firm and proceed as planned?

The same principle applies to the other life stories. We must be able to adapt to changing circumstances. The most successful people are those who learn when and how to bend. In a career, you may get a new boss who wants to do things a different way, or maybe a new technology is introduced and you are expected to begin using it right away. You must be willing to adjust, compromise, and adapt if you are going to keep your job. Maybe the third child born into your family has special needs, requiring more time and attention than the previous two. Your entire family will need to adapt to accommodate the new situation. Friendships change as time moves on; if you cannot keep up with the changes, you risk losing your friends.

Adaptability is a critical attribute in running and in each life story. As distance mavens, we must understand how our levels of adaptability and open-mindedness influence our success in all aspects of our lives. Equally important is the ability to know when *not* to bend. Adaptability must be tempered with the appropriate amount of determination and commitment to an original goal. Too much adaptability would be as damaging as too little.

Consider if Junior O'Tool were the exact opposite of how we described him at the beginning of this chapter. What if he had no spine and was willing to submit to any level of authority, yield to what other people wanted, back down under the slightest pressure, or surrender at the first sign of conflict? His life would be just as much a disaster as what we described.

> Adam and I had to adapt from me putting his running first to him putting my running first. That was a pretty massive undertaking. There was a time when I used to make sacrifices for Adam, and then it changed to where I didn't make any sacrifices and he was the one altering his plans. And then [our son] Colt came, and now everything is built around him.
>
> **—Kara Goucher**

So while examining yourself in Mirror 4, reflect on your ability to distinguish the need to bend versus the need to stand firm. The left end of the scale shown in the exercise represents the inability to know when to bend, while the right side depicts the ability to artfully find the balance between rigid determination and appropriate adaptability.

Let's start with running. As a runner, you understand the importance of consistent training, setting goals, proper nutrition, and all the other ingredients that go into getting fit and running at your highest levels. You have, no doubt, confronted obstacles ranging from significant injury to ordinary lack of motivation. Bad weather, illness, frustrating plateaus, aging, marriage, job, school, and family commitments all compete for your time and threaten to pull you away from training. Every day, you could find a reason not to run. Conversely, every day, you could choose to make running your top priority over everything else. Neither of these extremes is a healthy choice, and neither will lead to success in the long term. In your running, you must know when to bend and when to stick to a plan.

With the mirror exercise that ends this chapter, you will have looked into four of the six mirrors. Hopefully, you are developing a deeper understanding of who you are as a runner and as the hero in each of your life stories. Hopefully, you are also starting to see that these attributes and mirrors do not exist in isolation. Determination can be an integral component of responsibility. Adaptability can temper excessive determination. Each attribute is woven into the fabric of the others. Even though we are considering them one at a time, the complete attribute set, when considered as a whole, represents who we are and what we are like as runners and as the protagonists in our life stories.

The next piece of the puzzle, described in Chapter 10, may be the most important in terms of its impact on the other mirrors.

WAY of the MAVEN

Mirror 4: Adaptability

Think about your own running story, and take a long look in the adaptability mirror. Are you willing to adjust your time and other aspects of your life to get in your training? Conversely, are you willing to adjust your training plan when the weather is bad or other life commitments need to take priority? Can you walk that fine line between tough and stupid, where you push to be tough but are careful not to be too tough? Draw another scale, and place a mark on the continuum between the reactor and the distance maven to represent your balance and ability of knowing when to bend in your running.

Just because you are a runner does not mean that the rest of your life disappears or takes a backseat on the priority scale. You still have family commitments, a job, friendships, groups, and other activities that share a slice of your overall life. You must adapt each of your life stories to find the optimal balance to maintain high levels of success in each.

For each of your other life stories, rate yourself just as you did in the previous three chapters. Be sure to consider each life story individually. Do not be afraid to consider your weakest qualities. Are you overly rigid and unwilling to bend when it comes to being a spouse or a parent? Are you too compromising and submissive in your family relationships or with friends? Be honest to create an accurate reflection of your real self. Remember, this is just a baseline or a place to start. In Part 3, we will look at specific strategies for improvement.

CHAPTER 10

Get Real

INTEGRITY

I am not what I think I am
I am not what you think I am
I am what I think, you think I am
—Robert Bierstedt

"If you have a dream, believe in yourself, and never give up, then you can accomplish anything!" Audiences rise to their feet and applaud at the conclusion of a rousing speech given by a person who overcame great odds, broke through impossible barriers, ignored all the people who said, "You can't," and did it anyway. The story pulls at our heartstrings and, for a moment, makes us believe that anything is possible. The only problem? It's all a myth!

THE GREAT MYTH

The truth is, we can't accomplish "anything." We all have genetic and environmental limitations that mark the boundaries of what is possible for us. A five-foot-three man born with one arm and a curved spine is certainly capable of accomplishing many goals. Through his initiative, responsibility, determination, and adaptability, he can accomplish great things in a variety of pursuits and serve as an inspiration to others. But, if that man's dream is to play in the NBA, he is going to run into problems. If he believed the inspirational speaker who looked directly into the camera and told the world that they can do anything if they just believe and never give up, then he is in for a letdown. He could spend all his time practicing and could develop a pretty good shot and some good basketball skills, but the NBA isn't in the cards.

Likewise in running, it would be naive of us to believe that if we just train hard enough, focus, and commit, then we can all become Olympic 10,000-meter champions. There are other factors at play, and to deny this reality is to tell an even greater lie to ourselves.

Have you ever met a runner who imagined himself to be better than he really was? Have you ever met a runner who lied about her PRs? Or runners who not only lie to other people about how much or how fast they run, but also lie to themselves? Odds are, if you have been in the running community for very long, you have met a few runners who fit these descriptions. Perhaps you yourself have embellished the truth a bit, like an angler who adds a couple inches to the fish he or she caught over the weekend.

These harmless fish tales are not the focus of this chapter. Telling a tall tale about your running or racing can make a boring story more interesting at a party. If the real story is that at mile five, you felt a blister developing on your right toe and you confirmed your suspicions at the end of the race, when you took off your sock, that is a boring story. But if you enhance the story by describing the bloody footprints that measured your stride over the last two miles and the ruined shoes the medics had to cut from your feet and place in a biohazard container, well, this is just good old-fashioned storytelling!

This chapter is more about being honest with yourself. As simple as that may sound, it is one of the most difficult things we must do on the path to becoming distance mavens. Early in the book, we examined the notion of the self. We considered what the self is, how we refer to it, and how at times we perceive ourselves as being separate from us and who we are. The practice of lying to ourselves is so common because it protects our egos from having to face the reality that who we really are is a long way from who we wish to be.

Read the following list of statements. Nod your head yes or no according to whether you initially feel that it applies to you. Now stop and really think about it, this time being utterly honest with yourself. Then respond again.

- I am trustworthy and never lie.
- I am self-disciplined with my finances.
- I am loyal to my friends and family.
- I don't engage in gossip.
- I never judge people by how they look or their ethnicity.
- I always give my best effort.
- I always keep my word and my promises.
- I have nothing to hide from others.
- I never cheat on homework, on taxes, or on my significant other.
- I do not avoid conflict or difficult conversations.
- I never make up facts to support my arguments in a conversation.
- I am always on task at work.
- I never purposely try to hurt other people's feelings.
- I am a dedicated and thoughtful friend.
- I am always honest with myself about who I am.

> Being honest with yourself can be hard. Sometimes, people overestimate how easy things are going to be or underestimate how hard it is going to be do something. So when you fail at something, it can make it hard. When I have failed at something, I have to keep in mind that it was worth trying and that failure is OK.
>
> **—Dathan Ritzenhein**

Most likely, you had a variety of responses to the list. Some of the statements described you at first glance and still held up under greater scrutiny. Others seemed to describe you, or you would like them to describe you, but if you were honest, they didn't describe you to the extent you would have liked. This is a difficult activity. Part of being honest with yourself is to leave yourself vulnerable to the criticism and judgment of the person who matters the most: you.

The previous five chapters have relied on your ability to be honest with yourself. Your ability to get real and see yourself for who you really are, and not as you would like others to see you, is paramount to success in becoming a distance maven. If distance mavens are experts in self-knowledge and are empowered to change themselves in light of that knowledge, then they must possess clear, unbiased, and unfiltered views of themselves. Anything less, and the entire process is a lie and a waste of time.

BE GREAT AT SOMETHING ELSE

We know it is wrong to lie to other people. Our parents, teachers, coaches, pastors, and friends and even the mass media bombard us with messages about being honest and trustworthy with other people, but little is made of the importance of not lying to ourselves. Inspirational speakers like the one mentioned above even encourage us to lie to ourselves by believing that our capabilities are limitless. It is no wonder so many of us struggle to see ourselves for who we really are. Sometimes it takes a great lesson to force us to look in the mirror and see our true reflection.

Tim

The rest of my teammates had left the coach's office to go home and rest their weary bodies after an intense workout during my junior cross-country season at CU. I was the last one to pry myself from the couch to head home when Coach Mark Wetmore emerged from behind his closed office door. He plopped down on the couch across from me, looking pensive, so I settled back down, hoping to hear what was on his mind. Always a philosopher and deep thinker, I was captivated by how Mark's mind worked.

The conversation started with my thoughts on my own workout, but quickly swerved when I mentioned a runner who had done the first three intervals with me and then had disappeared on the fourth. I could tell this runner was on Mark's mind. It had become a regular occurrence for this guy to be having a great workout or race before encountering a twisted ankle, an elbow in the chest, a bug in the eye, or some other complication. It happened too often to be bad luck. It was a pattern of behavior, and it was a big problem. He was not just being dishonest with the team and with Mark; he was lying to himself. He was a runner with more faith in his abilities and inevitable greatness than his statistics or race performances would indicate. He was talented. No one doubted his talent. But he did not perform when it mattered.

I remember Mark's message well. "This guy is not hurting our team," Mark began. "We have nine guys to replace him. He is a walk-on, so he is not taking up a scholarship. He is harming no one but himself." Mark paused and then said, "But I am worried about him."

I was not expecting Mark to be worried. Angry or frustrated, yes, but not worried. "Each time he brags about how many miles he ran over the summer, each time he tells us how great he is when no one is looking, each time he allows himself to drop out and then come up with an excuse, he is learning something about himself. He is learning how to protect himself from having to follow through on promises, by telling himself and others lies. He is learning that he is a phony and setting himself up for disappointment." Then Mark looked at me with his typical challenging gaze and asked, "What have you learned about yourself?"

That conversation stuck with me and even haunted me for the next two years. I never wanted to allow myself to be a phony or anything less than authentic. I never lied in my running log or told people I was better than I really was. I wanted to be honest with myself about who I was as a runner and as a person.

The year after I graduated, I picked up a small deal to continue running through grad school. My sponsor would not pay me any money, but would keep me in shoes and gear and pay for my entries and trips to competitions during the season. Mark and CU were kind enough to allow me to continue running with the team and using the training room. In 1996, I had the B standard for the Olympic Trials in the 3000-meter steeplechase, but needed to improve to get the A standard and guarantee my spot on the starting line. I was full of hope and the runner's optimism and confidence. *Get me in the right race*, I thought, *and I know I can run fast!*

At the Mt. SAC (Mt. San Antonio College) Relays in March, I was in the fast race I needed. I was also running on a hairline crack in my left tibia. Twice a week, I had been getting a treatment called iontophoresis, which was supposed to be delivering hydrocortisone to the affected area of my shin through the use of an electrical current. I would leave the training room with tiny blisters on the surface of my skin where the electrodes had been attached, but I believed the pain was significantly reduced. Meanwhile, my doctor had advised me not to land on that leg when jumping the barriers or coming off the water jump.

Everything was going according to plan entering lap number three. I was on pace to improve my time to the needed standard if I could hold pace. On top of the third water jump, I realized that I was set up to land on my bad leg. I did a quick hitch step in midair and landed awkwardly on my good leg, but my right foot went instantly numb from the arch back through my heal. For the rest of the race, it felt as if I were running on a lifeless stump. I had no pain, but knew something was terribly wrong. Despite running a new PR, I still needed to improve my time to get the A standard. And unfortunately, my damaged plantar fascia tendon would not allow me to run a step for the next two months.

When I was able to run again, it was not pain-free. Each time I ran, my foot would revolt for several hours afterward, not even allowing me to walk. My fitness was continuing to deteriorate, but I thought I might still be able to race before the end of the season. Then I had a second conversation with Mark about integrity—a conversation that would change my life from that day forward.

One Sunday morning, the CU team was running twenty miles on the aqueduct trail known as Certain Death (the signs on the trail posted dire warnings to stay out of the water). I limped in after running a disappointingly slow fourteen miles and found Mark waiting for me. He asked me how I was doing and about my foot, but that was just a polite conversation starter for what he really wanted to say.

He asked me what my chances of making the Olympic team were, even if everything had gone according to plan and I had not lost so much training. We both knew the answer. At my best, I was still a middle of the pack runner more than twenty seconds off the Olympic standard and what it would take to place in the top three to make the team. I didn't need to answer the question. He then hit me hard with words I will never forget. He said that I was a good (not great) national-class runner who could hold his own in just about any steeplechase in the country, but that I was not, and never would be, world-class. He asked me to reflect on all the things running had given me, from paying for college to getting to travel and run in some amazing races. In his estimation, running had taken me as far as it ever would. I was not made of the stuff to run at the next level. His words cut my heart to pieces, but he was not trying to hurt me. He was trying to make me look in the mirror and see who I really was, and he was right. He advised me: "Go be great at something else." He told me to take what I had learned from being a runner and apply the same principles to the rest of my life. In a way, that day, he planted yet another seed that would one day become this book.

As a distance maven, you dream big, believe in yourself, and demonstrate the determination, courage, and initiative to act on those dreams to make them happen. But you must also have the strength of character to see yourself and your potential with an unbiased and realistic focus. We are all running the edge, pushing our limits, and attempting to get as close to our maximum potentials as we possibly can, but we must recognize that for each of us, our limits and maximum potentials are different. The edges we are chasing in running and in life are not the same for every person. What defines us as runners and human beings is not how fast we run, the size of our house or bank accounts, our level of education, or any other standard measure of success. It is how close we can get to our own unique edges or maximum potentials.

> I knew I was not in good enough shape going into the Beijing Olympic Games, but I didn't want to admit that to myself. I still thought I could just go—you know, the arrogant part of you thinks that you can just go and gut it out and maybe something will just click on the day.
>
> **—Paula Radcliffe**

MORE THAN A RUNNER

Adam

A few years ago, when I was dealing with the latest in a seemingly endless string of injuries, I began to panic with the realization that I was at a point in my career when I had a lot more good running days in my past than I did in my future. I was not able to run, and I was running out of time. My mind obsessed with thoughts of goals left unaccomplished. It killed me to watch other American distance runners toe starting lines at national and world championship races. The rotating voices in my head were relentless. *I should be there. I am better than those guys. I am a failure.*

Depression was slowly wrapping its tendrils around my mind and pulling me deeper into a dark place where I could not even look at myself in the mirror. When I did catch my reflection, all I saw was failure and disappointment. I would feel only slightly better when I allowed the depression to turn to anger, but the rage inside me needed an outlet and someone to blame. I blamed my coach, my doctors, and all the people who had lost faith in me. On a logical level, I knew that both my depression and my anger were not rational, but emotions rarely are. I could not see myself from any other perspective than my own. I would get encouraging e-mails and letters from fans telling me I was an inspiration, but their words seemed empty because these people didn't know the truth. They didn't know how pathetic I was. I would read an article listing my past accomplishments, but I didn't even know the guy who ran those races. All I could see was the current, worthless version of myself, unable to run, unable to shake the voices telling me what a disappointment I had become.

I needed help, and fortunately, I was married to an amazing woman who would never let me sit still or sink below the point of no return. She knew how to gently push me in the right directions and keep me working, even in my worst times. Kara knew and could see the real me even when I could not. With her support, I slowly clawed my way out of the despair and emotional wreckage of my mind. I permanently stopped visiting or reading the venomous words from the Internet message boards dedicated to running and was finally able to see myself as more than a runner. I realized that my identity and self-worth were not measured solely by my personal best times, number of championships, my lack of Olympic medals, or other people's opinions of my career.

In a way, it would have been easier to allow running to continue to define me and measure my worth as a person. But it was time to get real, look in the mirror, and discover who I was beyond the finish line.

It is still difficult to look back at my career and feel completely satisfied with my accomplishments. Some goals and dreams have not been realized. There are races I wanted to run, podiums I wanted to stand on, and medals I wanted to earn. I could still easily focus on these things and consider my career a failure, but when I look in the mirror and am truly honest with myself, I am confident that I did all I could with the cards I was dealt. Sure, I made mistakes. I came back too soon from injuries, entered races when I was not fit, and ignored good advice from doctors, but I never failed to give this sport everything I had. If anything, I tried too hard and crossed the line between tough and stupid too many times. When I take the time to reflect and am honest with myself, I know that I am not a failure. I am confident that I still have more to give as a runner and as a person. I am in progress every day, striving to be better and following the path of the distance maven.

Personal integrity can mean many things, depending on the context or who you are talking to. For distance mavens, it means being as authentic as possible. We have to be honest with ourselves even when the truth is uncomfortable. Knowing who we really are, where we want to go, and what kind of life we want to build flows from genuine knowledge of self. This knowledge can only be achieved if we possess the courage to look deep inside ourselves and face our deepest insecurities and shortcomings. But if we are following the path of the distance maven, we must look at not only our weakest attributes, but also our best qualities.

The epigraph at the beginning of the chapter is from a sociological concept known as the *looking-glass self*, the idea that we create our identities around how we imagine or hope other people see us. To get real and demonstrate integrity with ourselves, we must learn to view ourselves without this filter. The more honest we are about who we are, the more realistic we can be about who we are capable of becoming.

WAY of the MAVEN

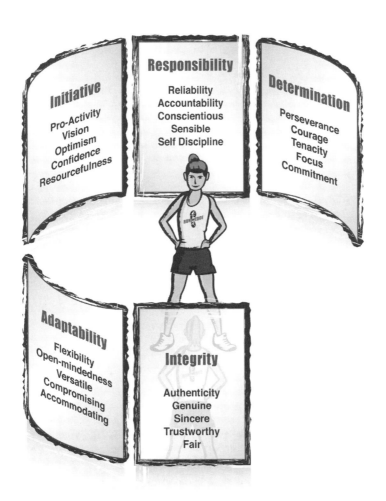

Initiative
Pro-Activity
Vision
Optimism
Confidence
Resourcefulness

Responsibility
Reliability
Accountability
Conscientious
Sensible
Self Discipline

Determination
Perseverance
Courage
Tenacity
Focus
Commitment

Adaptability
Flexibility
Open-mindedness
Versatile
Compromising
Accommodating

Integrity
Authenticity
Genuine
Sincere
Trustworthy
Fair

Mirror 5: Integrity

Choosing to strip away the layers of false bravado, naive optimism, and myopic egoism, you can finally reveal your true self. After looking in this mirror, you may want to go back and look in the previous four mirrors and ask yourself how honest you were. Did you rate your levels of initiative, responsibility, determination, and adaptability according to who you are? Or did you rate them according to how you hope you appear to others?

Rate your integrity, honesty, trustworthiness, sincerity, and authenticity as objectively as possible in each of your life stories. Drawing charts as you did for the preceding chapters' mirrors, similarly mark your assessment of these qualities in your running and in your other five life stories. To help yourself with this assessment, ask yourself specific questions like these: In your education, do you give your learning, inquiry, and curiosity your best efforts, or could you do more to expand your mind and grow? In your career, do you give your best each day and contribute to a healthy environment, or do you allow yourself to add to the problems and divisions between groups? In your family, are you the son or daughter you would like to be? Are you honest not only with your spouse and children, but also with yourself when it comes to creating a strong family unit? Are you the type of friend you would like your friends to be for you? Are you a person who honors your word, can be trusted implicitly, and is genuine in your relations with others? Do you give running and your other passions all that you have in a relentless pursuit of your maximum potential?

CHAPTER 11

Kindred Spirits

PERSON-ABILITY

Honor him. See the runner as the poet who seeks the pure viewing of all things natural, but in this instance, honor the warrior who sees no evil in pain; who feels no cowardice in tears, who hears no pity in that indescribable wail.

What a strange people are we, the few, the band of brothers who will lay it all out for everyone to see, just for a chance at purity; a chance to feel those goosebumps ripple as you feel him on your shoulder, while in the same second you feel your gait begin to open.

—Steve Curtis

We all need to belong. According to Abraham Maslow, who was discussed in Chapter 3, belonging is a basic human need. To be in the company of others who know us, understand us, and accept us for who we are feeds our social nature. If you have ever felt the isolation of being the stranger or the misfit, or the anxiety of feeling as if you do not matter, then you understand the importance of finding a place where you fit in.

Running is an exclusive club, but anybody can join. That is, you can become a runner and join the club if you possess the initiative to get off the couch and run, the responsibility to understand that there is no one else to do the work for you, the determination to conquer the hill and persevere through hard times, the adaptability to know when to bend, and the personal integrity to be real with yourself. When you are a runner, you are one of us, a valuable part of the collective *we*. You are relevant. You are part of a community brought together through common experience and shared passion.

> My high school teammates are still my best friends. I love them so much. I feel so fortunate that I got into running and it was based on having fun. I think you are the most honest with yourself when you are on a run. The friends I have made through running know me so well. It is crazy the things I have shared with people while out on a run. Things I would never share just sitting around having a cup of coffee. But you are out on a run, and you are just so open.
>
> **–Kara Goucher**

They might not understand *us*. They might yell *Forrest Gump* clichés at us as they drive by in their cars. They might think *we* are crazy for the way we love a sport that seems so excruciating. But we are runners. We understand. We are all brothers and sisters in this strange world, and you are one of *us*.

"MY DAUGHTER IS CRAZY"

Adam

Writing this book has been an amazing experience. I have been reflecting more deeply not only on myself and my own attributes, but also on what it means to be a runner. I am beginning to see running in ways

I never contemplated before, and this new awareness is showing up everywhere.

Recently, I was attending a high school cross-country meet. I was enjoying the fall weather and the purity of the sport I love. Several athletes recognized me, and soon I was engaged in some incredible conversations with several very insightful and passionate runners. As I signed a few autographs, I asked runners my new favorite questions: "How did you get into running?" and "What does running mean to you?" Their answers were thoughtful, some bordering on profound, and the passion each athlete had for the sport was invigorating. I am fairly certain I was getting more out of meeting them than they were getting out of me.

A little while later, I was walking back to my car when a woman stopped me. She had no idea who I was, but she had seen me signing shirts and must have figured I would be someone she could ask a few questions.

"Excuse me, sir!" she called from behind. "Are you a runner?"

I stopped walking and replied, "Yes, ma'am," trying to hide my amusement that she had called me "sir."

With an exasperated look, she came closer and asked me if she could talk to me about her daughter. I hardly had time to agree before she began, "I don't know much about this sport, but my daughter, Emily—you know, the short girl with the braces and a blue ribbon tying her two braids together? You were talking to her in that group."

"Oh, yeah. She seems like a great kid," I replied. I had no idea who she was talking about.

"Well, I am worried about her. She just started running this year, and almost every night since she joined the team, she comes home with a new complaint."

Her mom went on for about three straight minutes without taking a breath. First, Emily was complaining about her blistered toes and feet; then it was a turned ankle; later, sore knees followed by shin splints and at times just plain physical exhaustion after a hard workout. Finally, one night while Emily was going over her latest ailments and complaints, her mom asked, "Why don't you just quit running and do something easier?"

"And do you know what she said?" the mom asked me. She leaned in closer and placed her hand on my forearm as if she were about to confide a deep secret to a trusted friend. "She said, 'Because I love it!'" The woman let go of my arm and asked, "You're a runner. Now, does that seem normal to you?"

I smiled and tried to reassure this mom that her daughter's behavior was normal. I began to explain the mentality of a runner and how "something easier" would not appeal to Emily, because she likes the fact that running is difficult, adventurous, and sometimes even a little dangerous. She enjoys living on the edge, running the edge, and testing herself. The aches and pains of training are indicators that she is trying to improve herself not only physically, but mentally as well. She is becoming a runner and, in the process, learning that *just getting by* and taking the easy road are no longer appealing options.

As I finished that last sentence, I noticed that the mom's eyes were completely glazed over. As soon as I paused, she said, "So what you're saying is that she's crazy."

I repressed a laugh, smiled, and nodded my head in agreement that "crazy" was about the simplest way to put it. I resisted the urge to pour more philosophy on top of this already-confused woman. Instead, I just told her that Emily is doing something she enjoys and that despite all the aches, pains, and complaints, it is a healthy activity. Compared with alternative activities that high school students can choose, the mom should be happy Emily found and developed a love for running.

"But . . . she's crazy!" the mom insisted, as if she had not heard a word I said.

I gave in and just agreed with her: "I guess all runners are a little crazy, but we're crazy in a good way!" This was the first thing I said that she seemed to understand. She smiled and thanked me for my time and then asked for my name, e-mail, and phone number in case she had more questions. I gave her our Facebook and website information and told her she could ask her questions there and get better advice from the community than from me. Give her my number? Now, *that* would be a different kind of crazy!

In one easy-to-understand word that almost does justice to our passion, *crazy* sums up just about everything we do. Being a part of the running community gives us permission to be as crazy as we need to be. Running allows us to be a part of a collective, where the misfits, rejects, and mavericks all have a home.

Yes, this is an individual sport; no one else can do it for us, and there is nowhere to hide. But although we must take sole responsibility for our performances, the collective running community and identity is a strong and important aspect of the sport.

The bond between runners is built on common ground. It is built on the trails and roads we share and the suffering we endure. Like soldiers who are bonded through the intensity of warfare, runners are allied in the fellowship of exceptional circumstance and shared experience. We fight the same internal demons that beg us to slow down or stop. We purge the same negative thoughts and obsess on the same overpowering urge to discover our potential.

This bond unites us as a community. It is the reason we are able to congratulate a fellow runner as we gasp for air and struggle to remain upright in a finishing chute. The same runner, moments earlier, was a mortal enemy engaged in a life-and-death battle to the finish. The same runner whom we would have torn our own eyes out to beat to the line is now a brother or sister, built of the same substance, hardened by the same fires, and born of the same flesh. We would now defend this foe turned ally as fiercely as a mother bear defends her cub.

In the seemingly isolated world of the distance runner, we find critical strength in each other. We form training groups, join running clubs, and congregate at races. We are still alone in our responsibility for our efforts, but we are part of something larger than ourselves.

Psychologist Nancy Etcoff cites research on happiness that shows the use of the first-person singular terms like *I*, *me*, and *mine* are isolators and symbols of aloneness, whereas words like *we* and *us* are collective and show that we belong to a community. We are a part of something more than just ourselves. She refers to analyses conducted on the writings of the great poets who committed suicide, versus those who did not. The poets who committed suicide used these singular terms (*I*, *me*, and *mine*) more often than did the poets who did not kill themselves.

> I definitely feel that I can relate to all runners. We all understand the sacrifices that we have to make in order to train and achieve our goals.
>
> **—Galen Rupp**

In the running world, it is important to balance the *I* and *me* with the *us* and *we*. Being on teams, running in groups, joining clubs, and running races bring a vital sense of community to a potentially isolated runner. When we become a part of these communities, we discover yet another opportunity to uncover an attribute of ourselves and another mirror of self-discovery.

DON'T BE A JERK!

Being a part of the running community allows us to develop the sixth attribute of the distance maven, person-ability. The first five you can learn on your own, but this one can only be developed in relation to others. Imagine your five life stories again, and reflect on how initiative, responsibility, determination, adaptability, and integrity can help you in your education, career, family, friendships, and passions. Each attribute is a vital ingredient in the success cocktail, but to complete the attribute set of the distance maven, you need to add one more.

Being personable means that you are friendly, kind, compassionate, empathetic, considerate, and perceptive and that you have a sense of humor. Will having all these qualities help you in your education?

Career? Family? Friendships? Passions? It seems clear that this attribute is just as important as the others for overall life success. So how can you become more personable—that is, develop your person-ability—through running and apply it to your other life stories?

Tim

A former student and athlete I coached more than ten years ago recently sent me the following e-mail from Alaska, where she is working and taking the initiative to keep her life an adventure:

Dear Tim,

I went on an incredible hike yesterday, a 14 miler traversing three different summits. We finished in 10 hours. Somewhere along the way I shared that I would have been such a different person had I never joined cross country. We started talking a little bit about the differences between the experience you garner from an individualized sport like running or swimming, versus a team sport like basketball or soccer. We talked a lot about accountability, dedication, organization, a sense of self-worth, reward, empathy, humility, mental discipline, etc. I know this is a conversation you are having plenty of at the moment, but I always seem to fixate on a new facet of the matter and this time around I was really thinking a lot about developing empathy and humility. It was always striking to me on those bus rides home, when one athlete broke a significant PR and one had seemingly the worst race of their life. What delicate moments those were. They

> In my group, we are very honest with each other and we like to give each other a hard time. Sometimes, I am guilty of not knowing where the line is about giving people too much of a hard time, and I need to have a talk with myself and tell myself to back off a little bit. I don't mean to make people upset, but I have to admit that I was over the line.
>
> **–Chris Solinsky**

required some serious social maneuvering, right? I know we never discussed etiquette at these particular times, but I do believe that there was a more and less graceful way to conduct oneself that, though unspoken, was definitely understood. I believe this was a good exercise in humility and empathy because we all have experienced each of those sides at least once in our athletic career, and of course, by extension, our life. What a good way to learn how to be kind when others struggle with disappointment or defeat, even if you feel the exact opposite. What are your thoughts?

—Kris

Kris has it figured out. Because we are a community of kindred spirits, we practice kindness, compassion, and empathy. Most of us know exactly what it feels like to have a great race, a poor race, and even a disaster race. We know what it is like to be injured or to fight for motivation to keep going in difficult times. We have been there on that common ground that unites us, and when we come together, we practice social skills that will help us in each life story.

Much of our success in life is determined by the relationships we form and how we participate in and maintain them. Something as simple as being friendly and nonjudgmental can go a long way in clearing a path to success. In running, we build many relationships with kindred spirits, who, like our own families, can be more forgiving and therefore provide more fertile ground for developing our relationship skills. Most of us have experienced runners who are friendly and supportive and others who are less skilled in the art of being kind.

Adam

Being more personable is my top priority in my personal quest to become a distance maven. I am the first to admit that I have been rude, arrogant, spiteful, and disrespectful at times during my running career. I have damaged various relationships that are important to me. This is not who I want to be, and I am fully aware of the areas I must improve to become closer to my ideal. Although I believe I am kind and friendly 95 percent of the time, it is that 5 percent—when I lose my temper and say or do things to damage not just my public image, but also my image of myself—that I need to work on. I owe much of my running success, and much of who I am, to my coaches Mark Wetmore and Alberto Salazar, yet in my worst moments, I have not always been kind in my behavior or words to them. These have been difficult lessons to learn, but I am in progress and getting better each day.

In my family life story, I used to carry a lot of bitterness towards my father for not being more active in my life throughout my childhood. When we did get together, I was guarded and cautious of being hurt yet again, so I never allowed myself to get too close. But during my college years, my father and I started to re-build our relationship. I had to accept that he was a loving and caring father during my early childhood before a strained marriage and difficult life circumstances pushed me from the center of his life. I needed to forgive him and leave the past behind in order to be kind and personable with him. What resulted was a rekindled respect and friendship between father and son. Being more personable allowed me to enjoy a positive relationship with him for over a decade before he passed away from esophageal cancer in 2008. My family life story improved tremendously just by forgiving and being personable with a man who turned out to be a good friend. Rest in peace dad. I love you!

EMOTIONAL DEPOSITS AND POSITIVE REGARD

In *The 7 Habits of Highly Effective People*, Steven Covey describes the importance of making emotional deposits in our relationships. Even little emotional deposits can pay huge dividends when we invest consistently.

A kind word of support, a telephone call just to check in, a pat on the back for a job well done—Carl Rogers called these emotional deposits "positive regard" and argued that most humans are starving for it and will do almost anything to get it.

Tim

In my third year of coaching, I tried an experiment. I created a club called ETC. Like this book, ETC would use running as a metaphor for life and help us improve the quality of our day-to-day living. It was a teenage life improvement club for runners, and it became incredibly popular.

Each week, we had an assignment that lay outside of our running workouts and was designed to improve our lives and the lives of others. I explained the concept of emotional deposits and positive regard to the team and proposed that as a new club, we should work on building relationships in the school so that we could engender the support of the community. I gave the runners an assignment that turned out to be far more powerful than I could have imagined.

We made small greeting cards with our logo on the front and the words "Just wanted you to know . . ." on the inside. The assignment was for each runner to hand out a least five of these cards. The kids were to write something sincere and positive about a person they know and then give the person the card. They could give the cards to each other, their best friends, teachers, parents, or anybody else they wanted to, but I challenged them to also give cards to the school's support staff. I asked them to think of secretaries, counselors, janitors, cafeteria workers, maintenance crews, and so on. The runners could, I suggested, let these people know that their efforts to keep the school clean, running smoothly, full of good food, and operational were important and appreciated. I also asked the kids to give at least one card to a person with whom they had a strained relationship—maybe an old friend they had grown apart from, or a parent they were having a difficult time communicating with, or even an enemy they were fighting for no reason.

I was nervous about how this would turn out and if the runners would really use all five cards. By the second day, I realized that most of the runners were giving out an average of fifteen. I quickly printed up triple the original amount, and soon the school was flooded with our colorful little cards. I saw them pinned to bulletin boards in the dean's office and the cafeteria. I saw them on teachers' desks and in the library. I was thanked multiple times by the janitorial staff and the administrators in the front and back offices. But the most memorable experience for me came when one of the school's oldest and least-loved teachers stopped me in the hallway before school. I hardly knew this teacher, but knew her reputation as a teacher who did not like kids. She asked me if I was responsible for the ETC club. I nodded halfway, expecting some criticism. She reached into her purse with trembling fingers and pulled out a light blue card. She looked at me with watery eyes and said, "I want you to see what one of your runners gave to me." As I read the card, she continued, "I could not sleep last night. This is the nicest thing any student has ever given me. This will get me through three more years of teaching." As I handed her back the card, one tear finally escaped her eyes. She embraced me in a long hug. I was too shocked to speak.

After that week, there was not a locked door that a smiling custodian wouldn't unlock for us at the school or a special request for supplies that a cheerful secretary wouldn't grant. Some of the runners told me about their parents' reactions as they read cards thanking them for all the sacrifices, lessons, and love they had given. The week was very emotional not just for the people receiving the cards, but for those of us giving them as well.

In terms of success, being kind, friendly, compassionate, and sociable will go a long way in our educational, career, family, and friendship life stories. But what about running? Will being personable make us better runners? Although this attribute might not be as critical to a new 5K PR as determination, responsibility, and initiative, it can still help in running. Building relationships with these kindred spirits will make it more likely that we will have training partners, obtain valuable advice and counsel when we need it, and have shoulders to lean on when we need them the most. We cannot underestimate the importance of person-ability as a critical component of the attribute set of distance mavens.

Want a surefire way to lift your spirits on a day that you are feeling blue? On a day when you are prone to feeling sorry for yourself or to wish that someone would offer you some words of encouragement, take the initiative to help yourself. Spend thirty minutes of this rotten day to handwrite five cards designed to make another person's day better. Start it out with "Just wanted you to know . . ." and fill in the rest with heartfelt and genuine appreciation for what this person contributes to your life. Send off these five cards, and bask in having just used a small piece of your life to touch someone else's. Your day just mattered. You just made yourself more relevant in someone else's life. You just practiced compassion, empathy, and kindness. You just made yourself and the world a little bit better.

Up to this point in the book, we have encouraged you to decide whether you are the sort of person who sits back on the couch of life and reacts to things, looking for excuses to continue with "good enough" instead of pursuing the exceptional. Now that you have a good grasp of your own stronger and weaker qualities and how these qualities either restrict or expand your limits as a runner and a person, we will next challenge you to get off the couch in a different way. Part 3 will help you discover your own get-off-the-couch strategies for improving your life as a distance maven.

WAY of the MAVEN

Initiative

Pro-Activity
Vision
Optimism
Confidence
Resourcefulness

Responsibility

Reliability
Accountability
Conscientious
Sensible
Self Discipline

Determination

Perseverance
Courage
Tenacity
Focus
Commitment

Awareness

Being able to reflect and
understand the role you play in
your success and failure

Adaptability

Flexibility
Open-mindedness
Versatile
Compromising
Accommodating

Integrity

Authenticity
Genuine
Sincere
Trustworthy
Fair

Person-ability

Friendliness
Kindness
Consideration
Sense of Humor
Perceptive

Mirror 6: Person-ability

As you reflect on each of your life stories in this now-familiar exercise, think about your relationships in each aspect of your life. In your educational story, who are your teachers? Even if you are out of school, you continue to learn from others—friends, pastors, family members, co-workers, club members, and even acquaintances who teach us new things every day. How do you relate to these people? Do they know how much you appreciate them? Are you warm and friendly to them, or cold and aloof? Next think about your career. What are your relationships like at work? How are you perceived by the people you work with? Do they think you are open and friendly or closed and arrogant? In your family and friendships, do these important people know how much you love them? Do you take the time to let them know? Are you unkind to them, even though you love them dearly? Could you improve these relationships? In your running, are you part of a larger community of kindred spirits, or do you try to do it all on your own? Do you share your experience and wisdom with other runners, or do you guard your training secrets? Could you give more to the other communities that your passions tie you to?

Look in the mirror, and reflect on each life story, remembering that integrity and being honest with yourself are critical to the process. As you have done for the other mirrors, place marks representing your level of person-ability in each of your five life stories and in your running on a scale from 0 to 10.

If you are like most of us, you will see plenty of room for improvement in this attribute. Knowing where you stand gives you a clear picture of just how much you can improve your life.

PART 3
Elusive Happiness

Running long and hard is an ideal antidepressant, since it's hard to run and feel sorry for yourself at the same time. Also, there are those hours of clearheadedness that follow a long run.

—**Monte Davis**

According to the Centers for Disease Control and Prevention, antidepressant drugs are the third-most-prescribed medications for children between twelve and eighteen years of age. The only medications that outpace antidepressants for this age group are attention deficit disorder and asthma medications. For adults between twenty and fifty-nine years old, more prescriptions are written for antidepressants than for any other drug. Over 100 million new antidepressant prescriptions will be written this year alone. What does this say about us as humans? Are we attempting to medicate ourselves happy?

Babies are born pleasure seekers, quick to smile and eager to explore a world of excitement and wonder. They are discovering who they are and how they fit into the world. At that age, babies are given time and encouraged to develop an identity and a sense of self.

But as we get older, that zest for exploration and discovery is replaced by structured learning, homework, and adult responsibilities. Like the story of the slowly boiling frogs, our happy and optimistic youth can be gradually, even imperceptibly, replaced by anxiety, apprehension, and even dismay. We lose ourselves in a tangled web of societal expectations, roles, and obligations. When the self is lost and the identity consumed or submerged by day-to-day living, we recognize that something is missing, but we no longer know what that something is. The self we were creating is buried in our unconscious mind, unable to escape.

No wonder most humans want to undertake a voyage of self-discovery. The romantic notion of escaping social boundaries by heading into the woods like Henry David Thoreau, to live intentionally and bring to light an increased self-knowledge, appeals to our desire to re-claim our childhood and sense of self.

In reality, most of us do not have the time or freedom to give up everything, head into the forest, and find ourselves. So we fill this need in other ways. Earlier in the book, we read about adrenaline junkies who place themselves in simulated life-and-death situations to reveal aspects of themselves they could not discover otherwise. They, along with soldiers, runners, and other athletes, look for self-discovery through action.

Other people strive for self-discovery through deep intellectual thoughts and internal reflection. Philosophers, poets, monks, and other thinkers search for personal enlightenment and self-discovery through close and repetitive examination of who they are. They travel inward via *thought* rather than *action*.

As distance mavens, we combine these two methodologies of action and introspection in a balanced pursuit of self-knowledge. Running provides the action, sense of danger, and opportunity to see who we are in extreme circumstances. The six mirrors allow us to look inside and understand ourselves from an intellectual perspective.

Our voyage of self-discovery is measured not only by the miles we run, but also by how clearly we see our real selves and our max-imum potentials. Perhaps this voyage will allow us to reclaim that magical part of our youth, when we were delighted in simple pleas-ures and fascinated to uncover the mysteries of who we are. Perhaps this—rather than antidepressants—can be the medicine we need for a happy life.

THE CHALLENGE OF CHANGE

In Part 1, we threw down the gauntlet. We challenged ourselves to rise up and overthrow our own mediocrity in a personal revolution. We made a commitment to become distance mavens who will use the lessons learned from distance running to become excellent at everything. Distance mavens do not want to be normal; they want to be exceptional.

We began by looking at what it means to be a runner, the secrets runners share, the attributes that runners develop, and the bonds that runners create with one another. We looked at how runners like to do hard things, take on challenges, and live extraordinary lives. Running provides a context for self-discovery through action. We learn about ourselves by pushing past limits and testing ourselves in extreme circumstances.

We broke down the idea of an extraordinary life into five stories in which distance mavens want to create success and fulfillment. Leading an exceptional life means achieving optimum levels in our education, career, family, friendship, and passion life stories.

We looked at some psychological theory of the self from Abraham Maslow and Carl Rogers to further define the self and to outline some possible characteristics of an ideal self of our own creation. Whereas most people allow themselves to be created by accident, allowing luck to determine who they are and what they will become, distance mavens want to intentionally create better versions of themselves through thoughtful action.

We made lists of difficult things we have done, completed a checklist of desirable characteristics we would like to embody, and vowed to make *someday* today whenever possible.

If running provides an action context for self-discovery, then in Part 2, we added deeper thought to action. We looked at the action of running and the attributes it reveals in six mirrors of deep, honest self-reflection to discover our true natures. These six mirrors looked at six positive attributes of the self. By asking ourselves how we rate on each of these crucial attributes both in running and in life, we can gain an accurate picture of where we are in each life story. Once we are aware of these attributes, we can grow, change, and evolve into the people we want to become.

MAKING THE CHANGE

If you have participated in the exercises in the first two parts of this book, you have already spent more time in reflection and have already gotten to know yourself better than most people ever will. But what should you do with this knowledge?

Spiderman's uncle, Ben Parker, advises his nephew: "With great power comes great responsibility." Most of us might not be able to climb to our cubicles from the outside of our office buildings. But if knowledge is power, then our deeper knowledge of ourselves gives us the power to change who we are. In Part 3, we use the self-knowledge we gained in the first two parts and create positive changes in our lives. We will outline strategies for how to narrow the gap between our real and our ideal selves and identify ways to make the change a lasting and effective marathon rather than a short-lived sprint.

CHAPTER 12

Mosaic Me

I am an artist at living, and my work of art is my life.

—D. T. Suzuki

We are all mosaic works of art. If you look at a mosaic from a distance, you can see the big picture. Examine it up close, and you may only see one or two of the pieces that contribute to the larger image. Imagine a large mosaic work made up of small ceramic chips. They are different shapes, colors, and sizes. Any individual chip by itself would not give the viewer any indication as to the nature of the larger picture, but each chip plays a crucial role in defining the overall representation. Change the size, shape, or color of any of the pieces, and you change the entire work of art. A skilled mosaic artist pays attention to each chip to make certain it maximizes the beauty and overall appeal of the larger picture.

If we look at our lives in the same manner, we discover that we are complex mosaics. Our identities are not defined by any particular piece of who we are. We might be runners, rare-stamp collectors, employers, parents, and members of support groups, writing clubs, and religious communities. We might enjoy parasailing, love to scour neighborhoods for garage sales, or be die-hard punk rockers. Taken individually, none of these pieces defines us or creates a complete picture of who we are.

In different situations, various aspects of our mosaic identities are allowed to shine. When we are at home with our families, for example, the relevant individual pieces coalesce into one whole and give shape and definition to our family-oriented selves.

In Part 2, we examined six pieces of our mosaic identities and analyzed the role each piece plays in our five separate life stories. Like true artists, we scrutinized each piece, or attribute, to fully understand how it fits into our life stories. Now it is time to look at the larger picture. When we consider the pieces working in concert, their combined effect creates a much greater picture than does any one of them considered alone. We are more than runners, more than the roles we play in our jobs or families, and more than any singular definition could ever capture. We are living, breathing works of art, but we are not finished pieces; we are in progress, still creating our own personal masterpiece.

"THIS IS GOOD! BUT YOU KNOW WHAT WOULD MAKE IT BETTER?"

Adam

I make an amazing dry-rub seasoning for grilling steaks. Just about anyone who has ever tasted one of my steaks will tell you how good they are. After sampling his first tender morsel, one friend commented, "These steaks could change the world!" I think everyone (short of the cow) appreciates the delicate balance of flavors mingling together as the flames from the grill gently coax every last ounce of flavor from the meat. Yes. My steaks are probably what I do best, but you know what would make them better?

"This is pretty good, but you know what would make it better?" has been a consistent theme in my life and a running joke with a few of my close friends. Every time we find something good, we muse about what could make it better. I am pretty sure 3-D televisions and glow-in-the-dark Frisbees were our ideas for improvements, long before they became realities. This attitude does not prevent us from appreciating and enjoying the current, already good, situation. On the contrary, we savor every moment of goodness, thankful that someone has gotten this close to perfection without us!

When I take my first bite of steak, I close my eyes and allow my entire consciousness to be saturated in the delightful, zesty flavors dancing in my mouth. I enjoy the moment, but the minute I swallow, I think, "Maybe just a little less garlic salt or a little more cayenne . . ." I am pushing my limits as I "grill the edge" to see how close I can get to my idea of perfection.

From the grill to the track, this philosophy is always with me. Even after my best races, when I am well satisfied with the results, I imagine what I could have done better. If I would have matched an early move, let a rabbit go, started my kick a little earlier or a little later, then I could have run even faster. If I do a few more strength intervals or practice maintaining form when I am tired, I can improve my time and placing. It was a good race, but you know how it could be better?

When Kara and I bought our house in Colorado, I walked into the basement and thought, "This is amazing . . . but you know what could make it better?" A nine-month do-it-yourself remodel followed, and we had the basement I always dreamed about. Still, if I were to do it again, it would be so much better.

A few years later, Kara and I got into watching the TV show *So You Think You Can Dance*. We loved the nights when we could sit down after dinner and enjoy our favorite show. It was good . . . but you know what would make it better? Two weeks later, we were sitting in the studio audience watching our favorite show live. Attending a show on the dance tour or going to a live taping has become an annual tradition for us.

In the fall of 2009, Tim came out to Portland for a visit. As we reminisced into the late hours of the night, retelling old stories and reflecting on how well our lives had turned out, the familiar phrase popped up again, and the notion to write down our ideas came into focus.

We agreed that as good as our lives were, we should not rest on our laurels or become complacent and stagnant. As good as my marriage was, could I possibly do something to make it even better? As great and as strong as our friendships were, could we take steps and actions to improve them?

Tim started to go all psychology professor on me, talking about humanism and the human drive to give life meaning, find fulfillment, and become self-actualized. We talked running and we talked life. We talked about learning, careers, families, friends, and passions. We talked until the eastern sky reddened with the promise of a new day, and we made a promise of our own: to pour the same sense of purpose and commitment into improving our lives as we had into improving our running. To live the edge, to run the edge, and to make tomorrow even better than today.

The next afternoon, following a great run, we returned to the topic of the previous night. "So when should we start this project?" Tim asked. I smiled because I knew he already knew my answer. Nothing had changed since the day we rode our bikes from Boulder to Fort Collins. Whenever possible, *someday* should be today. We began brainstorming about this book that very night, as we enjoyed some remarkably good steaks.

Running the edge and becoming a distance maven means constantly striving to become more. We will never be perfect. We may never even approach perfection, but we can push our limits, move closer to the edge of our potential, and become a little better tomorrow than we are today. Good enough is never good enough. If we settle for who we are, we stop growing. We become finished products with no need to improve. The curse of normal and the chains of average will relegate us to a life we never intended to live. To avoid this trap, we must examine who and where we are in each life story. We must examine each piece of our mosaic identities and then ask what we can do to make them better.

By going through the exercises in Part 2, we have learned a great deal more about ourselves than many people do in a lifetime. We have scrutinized who we are by examining our reflections in the six mirrors and assessing how our individual attributes apply to our life stories. Now we are ready to put the pieces together to create a complete picture of who we really are in our educations, careers, families, friendships, and passions.

REAL VERSUS IDEAL

Beginning with running, we can develop an overall picture of who we are as runners by compiling the scores we gave ourselves for each attribute. For example, Tim gave himself a 5 in the initiative mirror, a 6.5 in the responsibility mirror, a 6 in determination, a 7 in adaptability, a 9 in integrity, and a 4 in person-ability. This is a picture of his real self in his running story.

Tim

At first, I was a little shocked to see how poorly I scored myself as a runner. The picture showed a runner who was not even close to his potential or edge, but as I thought about it a little more, it makes sense and explains why I am one of those typical aging runners who wonders why I can't run as I used to. My initiative is moderate. I only run two or three times a week, and if there is a reason not to run, I don't mind missing. I realize that I am the only one who can do my runs and get myself fit, but I am not as reliable or self-disciplined as I used to be in getting in my workouts. I am still fairly determined when I am on my runs, but since I no longer race, I don't fight as hard through pain and fatigue as I could. My integrity is high, as I believe I am very honest with myself about where I am as a runner. I know my best days are behind me, and I do not pretend to be in better shape or faster than I really am. The reason I scored myself so low on person-ability is that I do virtually all of my running alone. If I ran with others, I would be able to share what I know, learn from my training partners, and have a social network of support when I need more motivation. Overall, this is currently me as a runner.

Once we have a picture of our real selves as runners, we can identify the attributes that we can improve. Even in areas where we are having success, we can still consider what could make it better. When evaluating this ideal version of ourselves, it would be rare that we would award ourselves a perfect 10 on any of these measures. It may not even be desirable to reach this limit, as we can see from Tim's ideal running self. But we can always strive for improvement.

Tim

I realize that my best days as a runner are behind me. I know I will never create a new personal best time in any race unless I decide to start

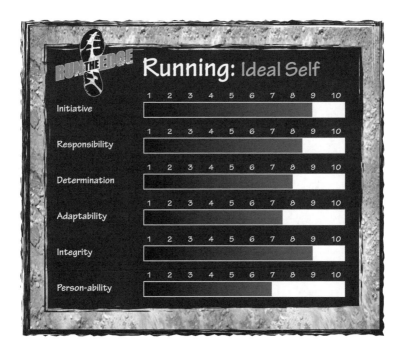

Running: Ideal Self

	1	2	3	4	5	6	7	8	9	10
Initiative										
Responsibility										
Determination										
Adaptability										
Integrity										
Person-ability										

marathoning. This is not important to me. What is important to me is that I get back into the kind of shape where I can enjoy hour-long tempo runs as I could when I was fit. I also want to take the time to run more often, get into great shape for my age, and reach out to include a few more people in my running story. My ideal running self is roughly represented in the "Ideal Self" chart.

When we put the "real" and "ideal" charts side by side, we see a graphic comparison of who we are as runners and who we would like to be. This assessment of our real selves is just a starting point. It is where we are right now. The object is to change our true selves to match our ideal selves.

As we can see from Tim's example, the runner he currently is does not exactly match the runner he would like to be. In the world of humanistic psychology, Carl Rogers called the degree to which a person's

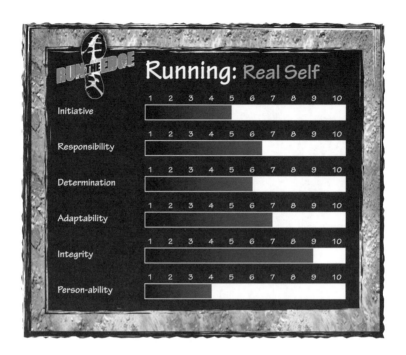

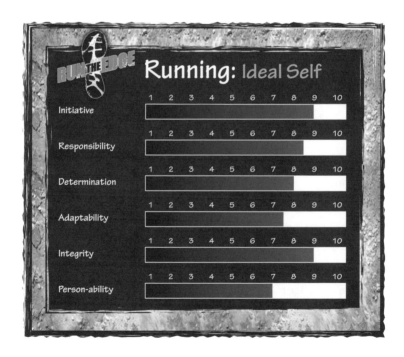

ideal self and real self match *congruence*. When our real selves and our ideal selves are too far apart, this *incongruence* leads us to feel bad about who we are. Rogers would say we are *psychologically unhealthy*. A healthy person, according to Rogers, is living to his or her potential. The congruence between who we are and who we would like to be leads to self-confidence, higher self-esteem, and general happiness.

HAVE-DO-BE VERSUS BE-DO-HAVE

Although this is a book primarily about practical ideas for becoming your own best runner and best person, a little bit of psychology can help clarify some of these ideas. As the authors of this book, we know that our thinking and attempts at improving our lives through running have obviously been heavily influenced by some of the heavyweights in the world of humanistic psychology. A fundamental and controversial assumption in humanism is that people are innately good and naturally move toward healthy growth and positive change. Given the choice, even people who are considered bad would choose to do more positive things with their lives than negative. The other assumption is that we are all empowered to change ourselves to become better. We are not locked into a predetermined fate that includes undesirable personality traits, unhealthy relationships, dead-end careers, and destructive habits. We are capable of changing and helping ourselves.

Change is hard to do. Staying where things are the same is comfortable and easy. Everything in my life—from changing coaches or training locations, getting married, to having kids—is hard at first. But when you jump in the water and embrace that change, it is almost always a good thing. If the change does not work out, you can always change again.

—Dathan Ritzenhein

The key to an unhappy and unfulfilling life is to buy into and live according to the *have-do-be* paradigm. Unfortunately, our culture and society teaches us that this model is the key to happiness. Our culture tells us that if we really want to *be* happy and *be* the best versions of ourselves, we first need to *have* enough things. We need to work hard to accumulate and have the material possessions and other stuff we believe will allow us to *do* the things our ideal selves would do. Once we *have* the stuff and are doing the things, then we will finally *be* what we are capable of becoming.

The problem with this paradigm is that most of us remain incongruent. The pursuit of material possessions does not bridge the gap between our real selves and our ideal ones. We are unhappy, have low self-esteems, and live unfulfilling lives. If we believe in the prevailing wisdom of have-do-be, then all we can do to *be* more is to obtain and *have* more things. We need a faster car, a larger house, a different spouse, a larger bank account. As soon as we have enough, we will *be* the person we envisioned in our youth.

This pattern can be seen in the prevalence of "retail therapy," whereby someone feeling depressed about his or her life decides to go shopping. Culture teaches us that having more will make us happier, so maybe a new watch or that pair of shoes we have been wanting will help us feel better. But as anyone who participates in retail therapy will tell you, any happiness provided by the acquisition of the new item is short-lived and does not change overall contentment.

The opposite of have-do-be is *be-do-have*, a paradigm that could not be more different. In this model, we first need to *be* the person we aspire to be. Put the final desired goal first. This is the object of the exercises in Part 3. Envision your ideal self, and begin the process of being that person. As you are *being* that person, you will discover that you are naturally *doing* the things that this type of person does and, more importantly, that you already *have* everything you really want or need to lead a meaningful, purposeful, and fulfilling life.

Mahatma Gandhi is often quoted as saying, "Be the change you want to see in the world." This beautiful sentiment has inspired millions to be active in creating positive change. We would like to break that quote down a bit and then make a small addition to it. When Gandhi references the world, he might have been speaking of the entire globe and all its regions and cultures. But before we can have an impact on that scale, we must first influence the smaller worlds we participate in. Our life stories can be viewed as miniworlds where we are attempting to effect change.

To have the greatest effect in the worlds of our education, careers, families, friendships, and passions, we must first *be the change we want to see in ourselves*. Once we are who we want to be and are living closer to our ideal or the edge of our potential, then we will find ourselves improving all those worlds without even trying. By *being* the best versions of ourselves, we are *doing* the things to promote the kinds of worlds we want to live in, and we will therefore *have* the types of lives others only dream about.

Runners understand what it means to be the change they want to see in themselves. Like mosaic artists, they work hard to create versions of themselves who are stronger, faster, fitter, and mentally tougher, in order to increase their levels of performance in their sport. They must *be* determined, responsible, adaptable, and full of integrity and initiative to *do* the things a runner does. When they embody these attributes, they discover what this sport gives back to them and therefore what they *have* in running.

Among the crypts in Westminster Abbey, there is an inscription on the tomb of an Anglican bishop:

When I was young and free and my imagination had no limits, I dreamed of changing the world. As I grew older and wiser, I discovered the world would not change, so I shortened my sights somewhat and decided to change only my country.

But it, too, seemed immovable.

As I grew into my twilight years, in one last desperate attempt, I settled for changing only my family, those closest to me, but alas, they would have none of it.

And now, as I lie on my deathbed, I suddenly realize: If I had only changed myself first, then by example I would have changed my family.

From their inspiration and encouragement, I would then have been able to better my country, and who knows, I may have even changed the world.

This philosophy meshes perfectly with the goals of the distance maven. We are dedicated to excellence in everything, to being better human beings and living extraordinary lives. Distance mavens are actively pursuing their own perfection and, in that pursuit, are becoming the change they want to see in themselves. In the next chapter, we will learn strategies for closing the gap between the real and the ideal, getting closer to the edge of our potential, and becoming the very change we are looking for.

WAY of the MAVEN

The Big Picture

You can now step back from the individual pieces of your running mosaic to see the whole picture. To create the mosaic of your real running self, go back to each of the six mirrors in Part 2. Draw a box with six scales inside, one for each mirror, and mark your score for your true level of initiative, responsibility, and so forth, on the appropriate scale. This is a visual representation of your real self as a runner. Now write a brief reaction or reflection, as Tim did earlier in this chapter.

Again consider these six mirrors in your running. Imagine how much you could realistically improve on each attribute to enhance your overall running story. For example, your running may not be the priority it once was, and therefore, you now consider a 6 a realistic goal for initiative. (Rarely can anyone award himself or herself a perfect 10 on any of the measures.) Draw another box with a set of six scales to the right of your "real self" scales, label it "ideal self," and mark a score for how far you can realistically improve in each of the six attributes. After you have set your goals and created a picture of your ideal running self, write another brief reflection. Your real and ideal running self charts should look something like those on the next page.

Compare the two graphs side by side to get an overall picture of your running story. The size of the differences between your real self and your ideal self represents how much work you may need to do to close the gap in your running story. Now you can repeat these steps, drawing side-by-side boxes for your other five life stories. Drawing so many scales does take some effort, but the big picture you create is well worth the effort.

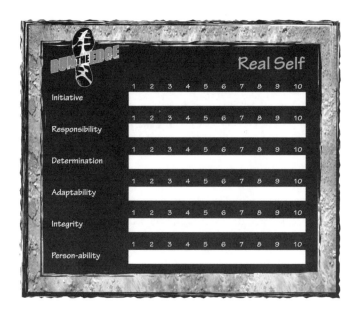

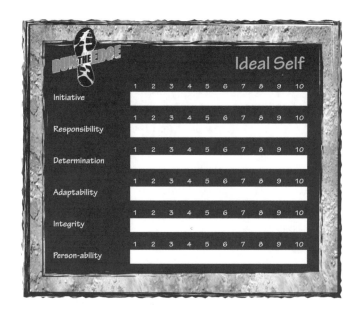

Developing these large pictures of your life stories will be important in the following chapter, as we look for strategies for closing the gap and gaining a higher level of congruence.

CHAPTER 13

Closing the Gap

Imagine that it is the final mile of a race. You have run as hard as you could have, so that your personal best, or goal time, is now within reach. You will need to dig deep to maintain the pace and achieve your goal. You look up and see a runner 100 meters in front of you. Can you catch that runner? Will you try? You begin to gradually increase your turnover, lift your knees, and drive your arms. You concentrate on keeping your hands low, swinging past your hips, and your eyes locked on the runner you want to track down. You commit to closing the gap.

SOMETHING SPECIAL

Tim

When a new student named Natalie walked into my ninth-grade geography class, I knew she was something special. As a distance running coach, I was always on the lookout for talented athletes, and Natalie was obviously a natural. She was thin, walked with a spring in her step, and had good muscle tone in her calves. Sometimes, these first impressions can be wrong, but she just had that runner's look that I had seen before. I knew that if I could get her to come out, she was going to contribute something special to our team.

After class, I pulled her aside and asked her if she would like to try out for the cross-country team. She smiled shyly, probably flattered to be noticed in the sea of over 2,300 students in the school, and agreed to give it a try. She came to practice the following day looking fit and fast. I introduced her to some of the varsity girls, who quickly welcomed her and helped her through our warm-up stretches. When the team captains were done leading the stretches, they signaled the group to run the customary two warm-up laps around the track before we began drills and the workout for the day. I was excited to see Natalie run for the first time. I was full of hope and confidence that she would give us that last missing piece to bring home the championship.

> Running has taught me how to focus and be right here in the moment. That helps me in everything I do. With running, I never want to fail. I set and want to achieve my goals. I am like that in every part of my life. Running has helped me want to give one hundred percent to everything I do.
>
> **–Amy Yoder Begley**

Over the next four years, I watched Natalie run countless races, workouts, warm-ups, and cool-downs, but I will never forget those first two laps. She ran like an arthritic moose in a swamp. With her head tilted to one side and a look of agony on her face, she sprinted to the front of the group and halfway around the track before she stopped, bent over at the waist, and gasped for air. It was as far as she had ever run, I found out later. And as the rest of the team jogged past her that day, my hopes for a diamond in the rough were replaced with feelings of guilt for asking her to join the team.

As she completed her first lap, clutching the cramp in her side, I told her that one lap was good enough for her first day and that she could stop. She flashed me a disgusted look and took off sprinting again, only to nearly collapse 100 meters later, unable to stand up straight from the exertion and the pain. The rest of the team members had finished their laps and went straight into their pre-workout warm-up drills. I could not take my eyes off Natalie. She started and stopped several more times on that last lap before she finally came to the last straightaway. I met her at the finish and put my arm around her shoulders to tell her how well she had done to finish the warm-up. As tears filled her eyes, my heart broke for this girl I had filled with hopes of being a runner.

I never expected to see Natalie at practice again, but the warm-up nightmare continued the following day at practice as she once again suffered through two long and grueling laps around the track. This time, the team waited for her and cheered her on and then waited for her to recover so that she could be included in the drills. It was not long before Natalie was able to complete the two laps without stopping, but she was always last. She started to participate in the workouts, or at least partial workouts, but always with every ounce of effort she could summon. She spoke openly about how much running and being an athlete meant to her, and how being a runner motivated her in other areas of her life.

> It is important to listen to your coaches as they can look at things from a more balanced point of view. That's not to say that an athlete cannot communicate with their coach and voice their opinion, but for a coach/athlete team to be successful, both people have to be on the same page and cannot do things on their own.
>
> **—Galen Rupp**

Rarely in my coaching career have I seen an athlete with as much desire or determination as Natalie had. As soon as her body could take the pounding without getting injured, she always chose to do the maximum weekly mileage and the longest daily runs. I divided the workouts into three general categories and mostly allowed athletes to self-select their challenge. I devised schedules for the "Rookies," the "Veterans," and the "Monsters." Natalie was no Monster, but she always chose this option. More than anything, she wanted to make the varsity team and stand on a starting line with the "fast" girls.

In four years of trying, Natalie never made it to the "fast" starting line. In fact, she was never close. She always ran in the open category with the other "slow" girls. In her early seasons on the team, she was always last, but as the years and races went by, she was able to finish closer to the middle of the pack in these races. She always ran to beat her previous best time, and more often than not, she succeeded. When new runners came out for the team, she encouraged and mentored them, never ashamed to admit that when she started, she could not even finish the warm-up laps. She gained the respect and admiration of every girl on the team and became a real leader at practice, demanding that the other girls give it their all.

In her final two years, her dream and ultimate goal in track was to run the mile in under 7 minutes. She said, "As soon as I do it, it is mine, and no one can take it away from me!" On a team where no fewer than ten girls could run the mile in under 6 minutes, this did not seem a lofty goal. But Natalie could not seem to do it. She would come so close, running 7:12, 7:09, and once as fast as 7:06. Each time, she would finish a race completely exhausted and eager to hear her finishing time. And each time, she would hear the first number of her time announced— "Seven . . . "—she would break down in tears, knowing yet again she had not met her goal.

In the final race of her final year in high school, Natalie was down to her last chance. I was not optimistic as she stepped to the starting line. I had seen her try and "fail" too many times, but two laps into the race, she was ahead of pace. Her head was slightly less tilted, and her stride longer and more powerful than usual. Her teammates, sensing how important this moment was and knowing how hard she had worked for this final opportunity, lined the track to cheer her on. When she finished lap number three, she was again behind the pace. She would need to run the fastest final lap of her life to break 7 minutes. The leaders of the race were far ahead of her and getting ready to cross the finish line, but all eyes were on Natalie. Her teammates were screaming encouragement. Even the sprinters, throwers, vaulters, and jumpers paused to cheer her on. She ran with everything she had, fighting her own genetic limitations and every impulse in her mind begging her to stop. When she crossed the line and the scoreboard clock had just clicked to 6:56, Natalie again broke into tears as she was mobbed by her teammates. But these were tears of joy, exhilaration, and validation for all of her hard work. I stood off in the distance staring at the stopwatch hanging around my neck, and wiping the tears from my own eyes to make sure I was seeing the numbers clearly. Natalie had done it, and now nobody can ever take it away. Through her own distinctive blend of character and action, she had fulfilled—in her own unique way—my very first impression: Natalie did indeed bring something special to our team.

Natalie's story is not unique in the world of distance running. The beauty and popularity of this sport lie partly in the ability of every runner, no matter how fast or how slow, to emerge a champion. Distance runners may not all stand on top of the podium, but like Natalie, they can stand on top of the world when they achieve a hard-fought victory against their previous limits.

Natalie was a champion, a pure joy to coach, and a symbol of everything that is right about running. She had her hard times, her fair share of frustrations, and her breakdowns during her four-year journey, but what did she learn about herself? What would Mark Wetmore say about her and her integrity? She wanted to be one of those girls who get to toe the line at the state championships, but deep down, she knew she did not possess those genetic gifts. Though her limits were different, she would not let that stop her. She didn't buy into the myth "If you believe in your dreams and never give up, you can accomplish anything." The "anything" she was interested in at first was beyond the edge of her limits and possibility. But Natalie was wise enough to understand that running was not just about who is first to cross the line. It is about who gets closest to the line or edge of their own maximum potential.

Natalie worked tirelessly to close the gap between the runner she was and the runner she aspired to be. She had to display uncommon initiative, responsibility, determination, adaptability, integrity, and person-ability to achieve her dreams. She had to commit countless hours every week for four years before she reached her goal.

As runners, we are constantly trying to close the gap: the gap between our current place and the runner 100 meters in front of us with a mile to go, the gap between our best time and the time we are attempting to run. Think of the lengths we runners are willing to go through to qualify for the Boston Marathon, break forty minutes in the 10K, or run a mile in under seven minutes. We will get up before dawn to get in our morning runs. We will train harder, eat right, stretch more, ice sore legs and muscles to facilitate recovery, wear Breathe Right strips on our noses and special socks on our feet, consume countless packets of GU, lift weights, attend yoga and Pilates classes, and even visit sport psychologists in our pursuit of our running goals. We are relentless in the quest for self-improvement, better fitness, and faster times.

Imagine if we went to the same lengths to improve our life stories as we do going after a new PR, goal time, or qualifying standard. Imagine how much better our lives could become if we applied the same levels of commitment, determination, tenacity, and creativity to improving our lives as we do in improving our running. This is the province of the distance maven.

The reason we runners are so willing to do whatever it takes to improve is that we can see and directly measure the gap between where we are now and where we want to be. It is easy to look at a watch, see that we just ran a certain time, and know exactly how much we need to improve to get the time we desire.

Filling in the charts in the last chapter has given us the same tangible knowledge of where we are in each life story and just how far we have to go to get to where we want to be. Just as in running, we now understand the gaps between our real and our ideal selves. Now it is time to begin closing those gaps.

THE LONG RUN

Adam

The second I crossed the finish line at the National Collegiate Athletic Association (NCAA) cross-country championships my freshman year, I started planning for next year's race. I had finished in second place behind Arizona's Martin Keino, but I believed I could have won. It ate away at me to watch Martin celebrate a championship I could have taken if I had started my move 400 meters earlier. After the race, Coach Wetmore told me to take a week off, celebrate, and relax, but I wanted to get started on my training for the next time I would be on that starting line.

I wanted to win that championship more than I wanted anything else in my life. To me, cross-country was the ultimate test of the distance runner. One starting line, one race, one champion. In track, these athletes would be divided up into the 1500, steeplechase, 5K, and 10K. I wanted to beat them all at the same time and in the same race. The thought of waiting another year to get my chance seemed unfair, but I was ready to train even harder and dedicate even more time and energy to getting myself ready.

One day, one workout, one ice tub, one good night's sleep at a time, I would put in the work and dream of redemption. How much better could I be in a year if I applied myself with discipline and consistent effort each day? I knew there were no shortcuts, but I wanted desperately to be on that line right now. I allowed that desire to fuel the day-to-day grind and felt confident I would be unstoppable the following year.

The hard work paid off as I cruised through an undefeated cross-country season right through our conference championships, when I injured the plica tissue in my knee. Every stride after that felt as if someone were poking a sharp knife under the inside of my kneecap. I went from feeling invincible to wondering if I could make it through the last two races of the season. I missed several key workouts as I tried every possible method of rehab and pain control. The following week, I gutted through our regional qualifier. Even though I won the race, my form felt sloppy and rougher than normal. I thought if I could just get healthy enough to run one more good race, I could finish my undefeated season, claim my title, and then let the knee rest. Instead, I limped through the final race to a disappointing sixth-place finish.

I felt as though I had wasted the whole year. I knew I was in better shape. Though I had put in the work, the championship I was stalking pulled away from me in the final mile and I was unable to respond.

Furious, I immediately went back to the same mentality that I had employed the year before. I would train even harder. I refused to take time off and was so angry with my knee that I decided to ignore it completely and run through the pain. I dragged that leg through every workout and race of the indoor and outdoor track season. It was a battle of wills. I refused to give in to the knee, and the knee refused to heal until I gave it the attention it needed. At the end of the track season, I had no choice but to have surgery to remove the plica tissue causing me so much pain. I sat out the following cross-country season to rehab the knee and get back into shape.

The summer before my third cross-country season was the best I ever had. I was training pain free and gobbling up the miles. I felt like a new runner and was ready to break the tape at the NCAA meet and finally celebrate the title I coveted most. I was again undefeated all season, and there was no doubt in my mind I would be ready to roll to the title. The day before we boarded the plane, I came down with a sore throat. I pushed back the panic in my mind and told myself I was fine. I could not be getting sick. I would not allow it. The night before the race, it hurt to swallow, and the congestion in my head accompanied the mild flu symptoms that made me feel weak and vulnerable. *How can this be happening?* I thought as I watched the three runners in front of me cross the line. I had been denied for a third time, but the familiar desire to start over, get back to basics, put in the miles, and train like an animal flooded my mind before we even left the course to head back to the hotel.

Three NCAA titles in track were already on my résumé as I headed into my final season of cross-country. As gratifying as those wins were, I felt as if my college career would be incomplete if I didn't claim a cross-country crown. I was down to my last chance. The story of that season and that race are well chronicled in Chris Lear's book *Running with the Buffaloes*, but what was on my mind heading into the final days leading up to that last race were the four and a half years of sit-ups, push-ups, weight training circuits, stretches, drills, good nutrition, plyometric exercises, ice tubs, massages, and visualizations. These, combined with all the long runs, races, interval sessions, speed training, and high-mileage weeks, had transformed me into a different runner. I did not sit back and rely on talent to get me through. I did not take shortcuts, give myself days off, or make excuses. I had put in the consistent work day after day, mile after mile. I was healthy, fit, and determined. I was also wiser and realized that given the level of competition with guys like Abdi Abdirahman, Julius Mwangi, Brad Hauser, and Bernard Lagat, a lot of things had to go right.

To this day, that race is one of the most memorable and most gratifying I have ever had. As I pulled away in the final 2000 meters, I felt a surge of energy and confidence and knew that it was finally my time. The race was taking its toll on my body and legs, but this was what I had been training for every day for the past four years. Finally crossing that line in first place put all my previous struggles in perspective. The fact I had needed to work so hard to achieve that title made it so much sweeter. I felt satisfied that all the work had paid off and that I could end my collegiate career feeling as if I had given it everything, not just in this victory, but in all my defeats as well.

The most important lesson I learned from that journey is that this sport and this life are long runs. Our ultimate success is not measured in a single victory or setback. Our running and life stories are bodies of work. I might win or lose this race just as I might say the exact right or exact wrong words to my wife. I might make a wise career move or a big mistake, just as I might strongly support a friend or do the wrong thing and let him down. These isolated instances are not what ultimately define us in any life story. It is the commitment to do the little things each day to get better. It is the bigger picture in our mosaic identities more than any single piece. I am proud of that individual title but even prouder of my cross-country career as a whole and how I was able to dedicate myself to the long run.

Runners understand that there is no quick fix. Most of us do not expect huge improvements as soon as we start training. We understand that to become a better runner, we need to put in the time and the work to build up our fitness slowly. We do our push-ups and sit-ups tonight, knowing they won't make a significant difference tomorrow. We set little goals to do this run a bit faster, to put in just a few more miles this week, to make sure we are getting proper nutrition, and to try to maintain a consistent workout schedule. Little improvements here and there add up to huge improvements in the long run. We can look back after such a year and say with confidence that we are not the same runner we used to be. We are much fitter and much faster.

Closing the gap between our real selves and our ideal selves in our life stories will also take a dedication to the long run. Life is not a 100-meter sprint. It is a marathon. We would be naive to believe that we can look at the gaps in our life story charts and become our ideal selves overnight. Just like a race, our personal revolution of rising up to overthrow our own mediocrity will not be won in the first 100 meters. Although we became distance mavens the instant we made the commitment to strive for excellence in everything, it will take time, consistent commitment, and a long-term view to get closer to our edge. To achieve that excellence, we must focus on one thing at a time. We can select one area, attribute, or situation to work on this week and commit to taking initiative and steps to improve in that area, and then next week, we will select another. Every week, we will concentrate on a different area of improvement while maintaining and practicing the previous ones. At the end of fifty-two weeks, we will have improved fifty-two aspects of our lives! That is vast improvement. That is transformation. That is revolution! We will become creatures much more of our own making than a reactor or tool of circumstance.

Tim

After looking at my running story, I decided that I wanted to improve my person-ability score to improve my overall running story. I had rated myself a 4 on this attribute, not because I was unfriendly or unkind to my fellow runners, but because I was doing it all on my own. I had no team, no training group, no running partner. I knew that if I did, I would run more often and get closer to my ideal.

I had just met a talented runner named Phil Latter while I was out on a lonely eight-mile run, doing my best to maintain a solid pace. He had turned onto the trail just in front of me and was running a very similar pace, so we ran the rest of the loop together and almost immediately became friends. We decided to meet up once a week to run our favorite trails around Fort Collins, Colorado. Phil was younger and faster than I was, but I could hold my own if he wasn't running below a 6:30 pace. Unfortunately, he had to do most of the talking, because I was out of breath at the paces he liked to run.

I took the initiative to get myself into better shape so that I could enjoy our weekly runs and participate in the conversation with more than two-word exhales. I decided to run two extra days each week. I knew it would take responsibility, accountability, and reliability to stick with this plan. I also knew I would have to be flexible and adaptable when something came up and Phil and I needed to reschedule. I decided to be committed to this schedule and make it a priority.

My friendship with Phil has motivated me to almost double the amount I run each week and has tripled the pleasure and satisfaction I get from my training. I have a kindred spirit to keep me going and to keep me motivated and consistent.

My running life story has improved dramatically with one small change in one mirror. I moved my person-ability score up one number and affected my running story dramatically. Can I do the same in my other stories?

WAY of the MAVEN

Small Steps to Revolution

Each reader of this book will have different goals, different ideal selves, different priorities, and life situations. This system of self-improvement allows maximum flexibility and self-direction. Your life improvement plan is unique to you and needs to be personalized as you decide which gaps are most important to close first. Study the difference between your real self and your ideal self carefully, and choose which life stories need the most work.

Remember that it is the consistent, small changes that will add up to create personal transformation in the long term. Also remember that being aware of who you are is paramount to your ability to change in the directions you desire. You need to take time out and look in the mirrors as often as possible to reassess who you are, where you have been, and where you are going.

To really close the gaps, you will need *initiative* to get off the couch and make small changes. You will need *accountability* to follow through with those changes, realizing that no one else can make them for you. You will need *determination* to stick with your plan, even when it is hard or seems impossible. You will need *adaptability* to know when to bend and when to stand firm in your goals and challenges. You will need to have the personal *integrity* to get real with yourself and know when you are giving your honest best effort and when you are falling short. Finally, you will need to be *personable* and find kindred spirits to help you in your personal revolutions.

The first three steps of a run are often the hardest to take. To get to those steps requires the commitment to set aside the time, change clothes, lace up shoes, and head out the door. However, once you have taken those initial three steps, the rest of the run flows easily and carries its own momentum.

The task here is to choose three small changes you can make in your life stories in the next three weeks. Look at your charts, and select a few minor changes that can have a large impact on your success and fulfillment. Like the first steps of a run, these small changes will show that you are committed and willing to put in the work. They will begin the process of positive change and start to carry their own momentum.

Maybe you just want to be more personable at work, or maybe you want to take the initiative to invite some old friends over for dinner. You might decide to pick up an abandoned project with the determination to see it through or decide to be a little more flexible with your family in areas where you need to bend a little.

Whatever you decide, commit to taking action by making one small change a week for the next three weeks. When those three weeks are up, take a moment to reflect on how those small changes have had an impact on your life stories, celebrate a little, and then choose three more small changes. Commit to the long run, and watch your personal revolution unfold.

Running has enabled me to apply that work ethic from running to other things. A friend of mine who I went to high school with is now working for a big law firm. He was telling me that taking the LSATs and studying for other law exams is so much like training for a marathon. You just need to dump your soul into it, and you can accomplish so much. It was so inspiring to see him transfer what he learned from running into something else.

–Alan Webb

CHAPTER 14

Alcoholics Anonymous, *World of Warcraft*, and the Mavens Guild

Tim

I went to an Alcoholics Anonymous (AA) meeting with my father the other day. At the time of this writing, he has been sober for more than nine months and continues to reclaim the life and the self his addiction stole away before he was ready for help. He was proud of the changes he was making in his life and feeling increasingly liberated from his obsession and destructive habits. I was proud of him as well. I had stood witness as he fought his personal demons. Having seen him under the effects of the disease, I was now watching him reemerge as the wonderful father and human being he once was. It was a pleasure to attend the open meeting with him and to share a small piece of his very personal journey.

Listening to the stories of these men and women was simultaneously uplifting and heartrending. They spoke in the most authentic voices about who they used to be, how far they had come, and the battles they continued to fight. One man received his sixteen-year sobriety chip that morning and held the attention of the room as he proclaimed that he had finally been sober for the same number of years he had spent drunk. He divulged that after sixteen years of sobriety, he had almost become the person he was supposed to be thirty-two years ago, when addiction had begun to alter his path. The silence in the room was thick during his lengthy pauses between thoughts. It was real, raw, and powerful. I think I understood what he was saying, but the other alcoholics in the room felt it.

I left that meeting even prouder of my father than I was before and intensely grateful for AA. This organization allows small groups of kindred spirits to gather together and dedicate themselves to the singular purpose of recovering from alcoholism. Individuals attend these meetings to find and maintain their own sobriety and to support others in pursuit of the same goal. It is a never-ending quest that requires constant vigilance and dedication. For most, fighting alcoholism on their own would be a losing battle, but with others fighting the same battle, people can form a powerful community and tip the odds in their favor to stay sober and to re-create their lives and worlds free from the coercive influence of alcohol.

THE POWER OF GROUP SUPPORT

Working together to fight individual battles sounds like a contradiction in terms, but Alcoholics Anonymous and other twelve-step programs have helped millions of people around the world by providing networks of kindred spirits in just about every community. On one hand, the task could not be more personal or private. On the other hand, the members must be open, and they draw strength from the group. Amazingly, the variation of ages, genders, social classes, races, cultures, languages, and professions vanishes in the common and passionate pursuit of a single goal. The barriers fall as people are united by a shared desire to improve their lives and help others do the same.

Running is a different kind of addiction. It can help *build* lives rather than destroy them. It is an addiction many people try to develop rather than break. But we can still learn from the AA model and piggyback on the principles that make it such a success.

Becoming a distance maven is a very personal journey. Every runner's story is unique and can seem like an isolated pursuit. Each of us must accept the responsibility and realize that no one else can take the steps to improve our running or our lives. Despite the solitary nature of our pursuit, the probability of success is low if we try to do it alone. If we find some kindred spirits who will take the journey with us, the probability of our success skyrockets!

If we want to increase our chances of improving our life stories, we need to fight the urge to do it alone. We need to find others who can share in our mission and who can understand the monumental challenge we are undertaking. Very few would think of climbing the tallest mountains alone, without assembling a team of other climbers who share their vision, passion, and commitment to getting to the summit. In the very best scenario, each of us can create a small, dedicated group of friends, or a *guild of distance mavens*, within our running circles to accompany us in the journey. Just like a small AA group, runners can find strength in community.

FORGING A MAVENS GUILD

When Blizzard Entertainment released *Warcraft: Orcs & Humans*, in 1994, no one could have predicted that it would transform into *World of Warcraft* and become the most popular, massively multiplayer online role-playing game in history. With over 12 million subscribers around the world, it has been nicknamed *World of War-Crack* by those attempting to describe its addictive nature.

Players of the game are immersed in a beautiful and dangerous world of fantasy, where they explore and take on various challenges.

(We would argue that these challenges are one of the components that make the game so popular.) There is always a next level, a way to advance, a battle to win, a village to raid, or a monster to slay. Players get to push their character's virtual limits, striving to find the edge of what is possible.

To advance in levels, characters must gain experience by completing quests, killing monsters, and exploring different realms. As they play the game, the players improve their characters' strengths and other attributes, making it more likely that the characters will encounter even more success in the future. Sound familiar? Although it is a game, it feeds into the human need for challenge and self-improvement. Imagine if 12 million people put as much effort and time into improving and advancing their real selves as they do into advancing their avatar characters!

One of *Warcraft*'s most important features is the ability to form guilds. Just like runners and alcoholics, players of *World of Warcraft* can choose to do battle alone, but their success will be less likely and more limited than if they surround themselves with like-minded people by creating or joining a guild.

> Teammates have helped me a lot. I came to a point where I realized that I couldn't train as hard as I wanted to on my own. In the short time since I have moved to Portland, having Dathan [Ritzenhein] and Galen [Rupp] around has helped me tremendously, and I hope that this continues to help me.
>
> **—Alan Webb**

In a guild, players can meet friends, share the experience of raids and quests, enjoy protection in fights, and accomplish things that would be unachievable if they were playing alone. If the guild is strong, the members enjoy the strength, support, and community in their online world just as much as they would in the real world.

Even the most diehard and addicted *Warcraft* player must occasionally disconnect and operate in the real world. Can individual game-play experiences offer lessons that will help a player build successful life stories in his or her actual life? Perhaps. But we can combine the principles that make twelve-step groups and *Warcraft* guilds so effective and apply them to our own quests as runners and distance mavens.

The path of the distance maven is difficult. The task of achieving *excellence in everything* is enormous. The likelihood of success depends not only on your own attributes such as responsibility and determination, but also on who walks that path with you. If you can find other runners who not only want to improve in their running but also strive for success in every life story, you can become companions and run the edge together. To borrow the term from *World of Warcraft*, we could call these groups of kindred spirits *mavens guilds*. The name does not matter as much as the opportunity to draw strength from a larger community and the increased probability for success. Fellow distance mavens will enhance your journey, help you fight battles, and accomplish goals you could not achieve if you run the edge alone.

By definition, a guild is an association or group of people who offer mutual aid in the pursuit of a common goal. The common goal of a mavens guild is improving the quality of the members' own lives through the lessons learned from running and helping others do the same. Like the singular purpose of AA, this is the common ground needed to unify the community. It is a dedication to a never-ending quest of closing the gaps between your real and your ideal selves.

Members of a mavens guild share a number of important characteristics. They are all runners who desire to live extraordinary lives. They want to break free from the chains of average and the curse of a normal life. They share a common vocabulary, can talk about their positive attributes, and understand how these attributes are affecting each of their life stories.

Runners are already kindred spirits who form intimate bonds with one another. Some of your best friends are probably runners, but if you want to take relationships to an even deeper and more intimate level and really connect in very personal ways with other human beings, try forming or joining a mavens guild. There, if you have the courage to expose the most honest and profound parts of yourself, as you share and listen to others doing the same, you will create cherished connections and have a faithful community of support.

Going back to the *Dead Poets Society* discussed earlier in the book, a mavens guild would be much like the students who shared a love of the written word enough to sneak away in the middle of the night to gather in a cave and recite poetry. Their passion for literature and desire to "suck the marrow" out of life brought them closer together and enhanced each member's experience within the group. It might sound a bit hokey to those on the outside or those who did not share their enthusiasm, but to each of them, the group was the perfect vehicle to further their quest and passion.

The greatest reward to being in a group like a mavens guild might not be in what you do to help yourself, but in the reaching out and helping someone else as that person shares his or her goals, shortcomings, victories and frustrations. You are not only the supported, but also an important pillar of support for others in the guild.

We know this might sound like a leap to go from a few pages in a book to forming a club or guild of runners all wishing to improve their lives. But if you have decided to join this quest for excellence and have come this far to run the edge, then a key component of your journey will be to share it with at least one other person.

So how can you find kindred spirits or forge these guilds? As long-time friends, both of us formed our own guild one night over Goucher steaks. All it took was for us to agree that we wanted to improve our lives and that we would help each other in that quest. Our group started as a guild of two, but is slowly adding members and kindred spirits as the journey continues.

Tim

Adam is a constant source of inspiration for me. Since the beginning, he has challenged me to push my limits, to mean what I say, and to give maximum effort in everything I do. As we daydreamed about what it would take to become exceptional in each of our life stories, I knew he would require me to follow through. Adam does not allow me to blow smoke, meaning that I am not allowed to say I want to do something and then act as if it was never said. If I say I want to get in better shape and run a bit more, he will tease me and question my toughness until I get out the door and do it. He does not tolerate my saying one thing and doing another.

Now that we are well into our personal revolutions, running the edge as we strive to improve our lives, Adam will hold me to my commitments. He will push, pull, taunt, and even shove me to make sure I am following through. I might be able to make some progress on my own with private reflection and commitment, but having a kindred spirit dedicated to the same goals and ideals that I am pursuing allows me to progress much faster and makes the likelihood of my success more probable.

> When I was a kid, I was in a training club with about fifty other kids, and I really bonded with five or six of them. And it helped me understand how to work on a team.
>
> **—Paula Radcliffe**

SAYING IT OUT LOUD

When you state your goals and desires out loud, they become real. Verbalizing your political or religious convictions makes them a part of you and your personal identity. When others know where you stand, you are held more accountable to your beliefs.

Adam

"I am going to be the first high school runner to run under fifteen minutes in the 5K in Colorado. I am going to win the high school national championship." These were just two of my goals going into my senior year of high school cross-country. In my junior year, I set the state record with a time of 15:03. I was happy with the time but thought, *You know what would make it better? Going under fifteen!*

I made posters with these and other goals in large print. They hung on the wall of my bedroom and were the last thing I saw before I turned out the lights to sleep. I told my family, my friends, and even reporters about what I wanted to do. My goals were written down in notebooks, hung on the door of my locker, and sitting on the tip of my tongue. By posting them and saying them out loud, I made them real.

I have been accused of being brash, cocky, and overconfident during my career. Some people have noted this as a flaw in my character; others, a strength. I have never been one to hide or suppress my goals from public view. Even though I have not accomplished every single goal I have declared to others, my sharing them with my coaches, my family, my friends, my teammates, and even the media has helped me stay focused and kept me accountable to back up my words. I believe that if I had kept my dreams and goals private, I would not have accomplished even half of them. I needed to say them out loud. Even though I would declare my goals to anyone who would listen, it was when I shared them with other runners that I felt the most impact. A stranger on the street does not understand what it takes to run a 5K or make an Olympic team, but runners are my kindred spirits. Proclaiming my biggest hopes and dreams to those who share an understanding with me always has a greater impact.

Now I am a distance maven. I will become better in each of my life stories. I will work with unrelenting purpose on improving my attributes to make the man I am closer to the man I want to be. I will work hard on the parts of myself that will allow me to be a better husband, father, and friend. I will strive to learn and grow both as a runner and as a human being. I will give my career in running everything I have until it is time for me to stop. Then I will work equally hard to be great at something else. These are my goals. I am putting them in print, sharing them with the world, and I expect to be held accountable.

Tim

I enjoy telling people I am a runner, but I do not readily share my past accomplishments or personal records. People don't need to know how fast I am, or was, to understand what being a runner means. To non-runners, it might signify that I am a little crazy or that I like pain. To fellow runners, it might mean I share a passion and some insight with them. To me, it means a whole lot more. To me, being a runner represents an important aspect of myself. Running does not define me completely, but it influences who I am and how I see the world.

I am a distance maven. I will not settle for average or accept good enough in my life. I will not rest on my laurels or believe that I am as good as I will ever get. I know I can always make it better as I search for my edge, my limits, and my potential. I can see that in my life stories, there is a lot of room to grow. My real self and ideal self are not the same, and I will take steps to bring them closer to congruence. I am a runner and a maven, and I will tell anyone who will listen.

If you really want to transform your life and achieve excellence in everything, then you cannot be shy or reticent to say it out loud. Start by looking in the mirror and saying, "I am a runner." Let that sink in for a few minutes, and reflect on what that means. Then consider how serious you are about knowing yourself and improving your life stories, and proclaim, "I am a maven."

It is not enough to say it to the mirror, your dog, or your houseplants. It will be far more effective to say it to kindred spirits and other people who will hear and understand your quest. You need to say it to somebody who cares, somebody who matters, somebody who will support you. At best, you can say it in person to fellow runners or your mavens guild. You can also go to our "Run the Edge" website at www.runtheedge.com and proclaim it there. On this site, we have formed the first-ever online Mavens Guild, which will hopefully serve as support for other pilgrims on this quest and as a place for distance mavens to find one another to form smaller groups in their own communities.

Being around other mavens and kindred spirits who understand what you are doing and what it takes to break the chains of average is the first step. Stating your goals and aspirations out loud in front of those kindred spirits holds you accountable. When you come back or meet with them again, you can say, "Here is what I have done. Here is where I succeeded, and here is where I failed."

COMMON GROUND

Recovering alcoholics, diehard *World of Warcraft* players, and distance mavens seem to have little in common on the surface. Alcoholics are trying to escape from addiction, whereas runners are enjoying their habit. *Warcraft* players participate in a quest to improve their avatar selves, but runners work hard to improve their real selves.

The common ground that all three groups share is the strength in community, the support of kindred spirits, and the increased probability of success when they take the journey with others rather than attempting to do it all on their own.

But no matter how important the community or how much strength you draw from it, you must ultimately be responsible for your own life and have the self-discipline and determination to initiate whatever is necessary to achieve your goals. You must unleash the maven on the real world as you strive to make the little improvements that will close the gap and add up to big changes in the long run.

Whether you are a member of a twelve-step program, a Warcraft player, or a distance maven, you start your journey with these small steps, not knowing where it will ultimately lead you. But distance mavens realize that the journey never ends. The joy is not in the destination but in the getting there. In the next chapter, we will show you ways to find that joy and what it really means to live "happily ever after."

WAY of the MAVEN

Finding Kindred Spirits

Hopefully, this chapter has illustrated the importance of sharing this journey with others and in drawing strength from a community of like-minded individuals. Maybe you already have a strong network of runners you can invite to run the edge, or maybe you need to branch out to find new kindred spirits. The following three suggestions can help you find and build mavens guilds or other networks.

1. Begin with your existing running friends and training partners. Find those who may be interested, and talk to them about life, their goals, and their dreams. Start an authentic conversation about running the edge and personal revolution. If they share your desire for self-improvement and are willing to continue the conversation and perhaps join you in the journey, then you have already found your support.

2. If you do not already belong to a running group or know any training partners who might want to share the journey with you and others, go to your local running store and find out which running groups exist, and inquire about creating your own. Ask if the running store will help you advertise in the store your interest in forming a mavens guild (maybe the store will even offer members a discount on shoes and other merchandise!).

3. Visit our website at www.runtheedge.com and search our community site for maven guilds that might already be located in your area. If there isn't one, post an invitation to begin one, and be prepared to meet up with kindred spirits and the best

friends you have yet to meet. Post a date, time, and location of your first meeting, and start to build your own community.

4. There are other online resources like meet-up groups and even Craigslist advertisements that can work to help find kindred running spirits. Be careful to choose safe and public meeting places when agreeing to run with new people. A ten mile trail run in the mountains might not be the ideal first run with someone you just met. Ideally you can form a small group and start to build meaningful and rewarding friendships together.

CHAPTER 15

Once Upon a Time and Happily Ever After

We all have a story to tell. We all can relate an account of how we came to be in this place, doing these things, with these people. Our stories are filled with moments of triumph, pure joy, hope, excitement, and wonder. They are also full of moments of despair, tragedy, heartbreak, and failure. Obstacles both real and imagined have impeded our progress, altered our course, and helped shape who we are. Even though no two stories are the same and we have all wandered different paths to get to where we are in our lives, all our life stories began with "once upon a time." That is, we set out on a path without knowing what lay ahead or if we would have a "happily ever after."

ONCE UPON A TIME: THE BEN DAVIS STORY

Once upon a time, there was a boy named Ben Davis. Like most children, Ben loved to play outside, run, explore, and imagine. He was happy, full of life, and eager to participate in a world where anything seemed possible. Ben was full of the same energy, innocence, and exuberance of youth shared by most healthy children. He was normal, but not yet bound by the chains of average. The future was wide open and full of possibilities.

"Then," Ben described, "I started to get big. So big that I became sad." A combination of genetics, a poor diet, and a lack of exercise sent Ben's weight spiraling out of control. As his weight went up, his confidence and self-esteem went down. The energy and exuberance of his youth were replaced by lethargy and a sense of hopelessness. He no longer enjoyed life and did not respect the man he had become.

By the time Ben was twenty-three years old, he weighed over 360 pounds. A doctor informed him that if he maintained this lifestyle, Ben's own father would outlive him. These were the darkest days for Ben. His *once upon a time* was not heading for a *happily ever after*, and he needed to make a change. Ben realized that at twenty-three, he was not the man he had expected to be when he was a young boy. To make that little boy's dreams come true and to be sure he grew up to be the kind of man he was capable of becoming, the adult Ben would have to take action.

On Christmas Eve 2008, Ben's grandmother, whom he affectionately refers to as Meemaw, asked him if he was happy. Ben lied and assured Meemaw that everything was great. But as he lay awake that night, her question haunted him: "Was I happy?" Two years later, Ben recounted the incident on his blog: "Of course I wasn't. I knew I wasn't. I had known for a year, at least. It had been, by far, the worst year of my life. I lost Tara [his girlfriend], stopped hanging out with my friends, gambled way too much, and spent the entire year locked in my room playing video games."

Ben needed to rise up in a personal revolution and fight to create a life worth living. So one day, he did something extraordinary for a person of his size. He ran. He made Meemaw a Christmas Day promise to get his life and weight under control. He started a blog called "Ben Does Life" to share his journey with Meemaw and anyone else who wanted to follow along, and on January 7, 2009, Ben and his brother Jed went to a local indoor track to see how far they could run. "I made it almost eight minutes before I nearly passed out," Ben recalled.

Almost immediately, Ben started to feel better. He did not have to wait until he lost a specific amount of weight to reclaim his happiness and purpose. As bad as it hurt to run, and as hard as it was to limit his food intake, Ben had made a decision and took the initiative to improve his life. He went from being a reactor to an actor. He felt a surge of self-confidence and satisfaction every time he finished a workout.

But his journey would not be easy. He had to work on the six key attributes that we looked at in Part 2. It took tremendous *initiative* to get off the couch and out the front door for a run. It took self-discipline and *responsibility* to follow through on his commitment and realize that no one else could do it for him. Tough times, sore muscles, and fatigue would test his *determination* and tenacity. He needed *adaptability*, as he modified not only his exercise routine but also his dietary habits to eat less and focus on healthier foods. He had to be real with himself and have the *integrity* to understand that he would need to commit to the long term and slowly close the gap between his real and his ideal self.

Ben also took advantage of his *person-ability*. He had kindred spirits in his father John Davis and his brother Jed, both of whom accompanied him during his journey, running many workouts and races right beside him. Ben also declared his goals out loud to others. In addition to telling Meemaw and the rest of his family, he shared his goals with the ever-growing list of followers on his blog. He had created an online support group or guild, and the likelihood of his success skyrocketed as he was supported by kindred spirits from all over the world. The realization that he was moving in a positive direction was all Ben needed to turn the corner and begin running the edge to a better life and a happier self.

Today, Ben has lost over 130 pounds and has run numerous marathons, triathlons, and even an Ironman! His life was back on track the moment he decided to be an actor and direct his own life instead of letting it happen to him. He took control and embarked on a personal revolution that would change not only his life, but also the lives of everyone who knows him.

Once upon a time, there was a little boy named Ben Davis. He believed he would have a bright future and live a happy life. For a while, it seemed his dreams would not come true, but the adult Ben has fought hard and is running the edge to ensure that this boy reaches his potential and lives the kind of life he deserves. When Ben was young, his parents and his grandmother hoped that he would grow up to be happy, healthy, and successful. Thanks to his initiative, responsibility, determination, adaptability, integrity, and person-ability, he has taken control of his life and grown up to be a man whom his entire family and the little boy he was *once upon a time* can be proud of. You can see a video of Ben's story at www.bendoeslife.com.

Ben's powerful story provides a great example of what is possible when we stop just reacting to the situation and rise up to take control of our lives. His story is vivid, tangible, inspirational, and emotional.

We all started out as little boys or little girls once upon a time. We owe it to those younger versions of ourselves to create the kinds of lives we dreamed of in our youth. Our stories are every bit as vivid, tangible, inspirational, and emotional as Ben's. All of us have obstacles and challenges standing in our way. We can choose to live passively, or we can live actively and direct our lives with intention.

George Sheehan once described the personal revelation he derived from running: "reaching a fitness which reveals the real person inside my body (just [as] the sculptor find[s] the statue inside the stone)." Ben's story is a literal revelation as running and proper nutrition melted away the pounds to uncover a stronger, more confident, and happier man. He revealed the man he could be physically, mentally, and emotionally. As runners, we easily identify with this story because we are also running the edge and becoming the true works of art we were always supposed to be, once upon a time.

HAPPILY EVER AFTER

Senioritis is a disease most high school students contract at some point during their final year. Some get it as early as September and begin infecting their classmates right away. By April, nearly the entire population of high school seniors is suffering from the classic symptoms: a lack of motivation, a desire to be completely done with high school, an almost pathological fear of learning new things, a decreasing interest in personal hygiene, and an increasing desire to spend enormous amounts of time wasting time. There is no vaccine for senioritis; graduation is the only cure.

> Running brings purpose to my life. That is the biggest gift that running has given me. When I wake up every single day, I am thinking, "How am I going to get the best out of myself?"
>
> **−Alan Webb**

Senioritis is caused by another of society's great myths. In Chapter 10, we looked at the myth "if you work hard enough, you can accomplish anything," but the myth that leads to senioritis is perhaps even more dangerous: the myth of "happily ever after." This myth leads us to believe that as soon as we accomplish a task, pass a milestone, or overcome an obstacle, life will suddenly be perfect. Children's books, Hollywood movies, and fairy tales reinforce the idea that once the princess meets Prince Charming, once the village is saved from certain destruction, once the hero slays the dragon, everyone lives happily ever after. We never hear or read about what comes next, but believe that they never have to struggle again.

Tim

I don't remember the class where the discussion first started, but it became a consistent theme I liked to discuss with my students year after year. I gave the speech, which I called "Wishing It Away," whenever I noticed that my seniors were starting to fall under the influence of apathy and inertia. I knew that a full-blown epidemic of senioritis was right around the corner, and even though my speech and the discussion that followed did not prevent senioritis, it did provide some awareness of a larger problem.

"Don't wish it away!" I would implore my students. "Enjoy the ride, the moment, and the process, because you will never be here again." The purpose of the speech was to have students consider that if they wished away this year of their lives, biding their time until graduation, then they would have bought into the myth of happily ever after. I would go through all the rites of passage and other key milestones people wait for in the belief that they will finally have their happily ever after. When they graduate, when they get a job, when they get a promotion, when they get married, when they have children, when their children are out of the house, when they retire—these are just a few of the life events people wait for and, in the process, wish away days, weeks, and even years of their lives. What they fail to understand is that waiting for life to get better is not how you find happily ever after. Happily ever after lives in the moments between those milestones and in having direction and purpose.

I would close my talk with a challenge: "You have a choice. You have to keep making this choice during every phase of your life. You can choose to wish away the moment or thrive in it. You can disregard today, focusing on better days ahead, or you can make *these* the days to remember. You are in high school. These are the best days of your life! Enjoy them. When you graduate, you will probably go on to college or start a career. That is the next phase of your life, and those will also be the best days of your life. They have to be. The alternative is to always be focused on a different time from now, waiting and believing in happily ever after."

I would like to believe that my speech had a significant effect on my students, but honestly, I was never a match for the more powerful influence of senioritis and the promise of greater freedom and a better life on the other side of graduation. But the idea of wishing it away was now something we could talk about and something students could think about every time they found themselves looking too far forward. It was also a great reminder for me as a teacher looking forward to the more relaxing summer months. It also reminded me that I needed to focus on making each moment count and creating the best days of my own life.

Happily ever after is something we have to create every day. Ben Davis started living happily ever after the moment he decided to get his life and weight under control. He did not have to wait to lose a certain amount or to finish a specific race in a specific time. The moment his promise to Meemaw gave him direction and purpose, his life turned around and he began living his happily ever after, every day.

It is the same for distance mavens. The moment we accept the gauntlet and the challenge of improving each of our five life stories in a quest for excellence in everything, we begin living happily ever after. We stop waiting for the next milestone or another event to bring us happiness, and we begin to create lives in the pursuit of a goal. The satisfaction and relief we get from achieving that goal is not permanent. We would be naive to assume that as soon as we break a certain time barrier in the 5K, we will be happy for the rest of our lives. Instead, we create new goals, new edges or horizons to chase, in a never-ending pursuit of a better version of ourselves. This is where happily ever after lives and the cure for wishing it away.

Adam

I am a brand-new father. The birth of my son, Colton Mirko Goucher, was one of the most surreal and impactful events of my life. This transformational experience made me realize that I no longer was living just for myself. Before his birth, Kara and I were able to allow ourselves to be our own top priorities. We could be selfish with our time, money, and decisions without hurting anyone else. The moment Colt came into our lives, neither of us wanted or needed to be selfish anymore.

Colt's once upon a time is just beginning. I would literally do anything in my power to make sure he has a bright and happy future. Right now, Colt is powerless. He depends on us for his every need. Fortunately, his current needs are limited to sleep, food, dry diapers, and love. As he grows, his needs will expand, as will his power to influence his own life. His happily ever after will slowly slip out of our hands and will fall into his own. I can't wait to watch him discovering the world, himself, and how he fits into that world. I am determined to guide him, empower him, and support him as he grows into a man. Eventually, he will venture into the world on his own. Our hopes and dreams, just like those of most parents, are that Colt goes on to live a happy and productive life. We hope he develops the attributes that will make him successful and able to create his own happily ever after in each of his life stories.

As I contemplate these things, I can't help but ponder the fact that once upon a time, I was this small. Once upon a time, I depended on my parents to feed, clothe, change, and love me. Their hopes for my life were probably much the same as mine are for Colt. Although we had our hard times and, during my adolescence, occasionally strained relationships, I am thankful to have had parents who loved and cared for me and my sisters to help us grow into the people we were meant to be. I am also thankful that I was able to reconcile with my father and enjoy several years of a positive relationship with him before he passed away in 2008. I know now just how much responsibility, care, and affection my parents put into my once upon a time, and I hope to make my late father and my loving mother proud of the happily ever after I am creating.

Colt's birth has changed my life in ways I cannot express. Long before Colt, I discovered running and experienced the gift that would lead to many of the best memories and days of my life. That gift carried me for years before I met Kara and added her as a best friend and companion. Life was even better as I enjoyed both running and being married to my soul mate. Now Colt is here, and I am still married to Kara, and I am still able to run! These truly are the best days of my life, and I am determined not to wish them away as I look forward to the next phase. I will work hard on my own life and on being the best father and husband I can be. I will be simultaneously creating my daily happily ever after and enjoying Colt's once upon a time.

WAY of the MAVEN

Childhood Wishes

Think back to when you were a child. Start when you were very small and completely dependent on your parents for your care. Your story was just beginning. As your parents held you in their arms, what do you imagine their hopes and dreams were for your future? Now imagine that you are a little older and beginning to discover things on your own. Envision where you used to play. Remember what it was like to be that young with your entire life in front of you. This is your once upon a time. If you could go back in time and meet that previous version of yourself, what advice would you give? What would you warn that child to avoid? How would you encourage yourself to enjoy each step of the journey and not to wish it away until better days happen?

As you take the first steps in your personal revolution, make a commitment to enjoy the journey. Remember that it is not the destination that is important. There will always be another edge or horizon to chase. What is important is that you are moving in the right direction with intent and purpose. Ben Davis turned his life around the moment he took action to change. He did not need to wait to achieve a specific goal to begin living happily ever after. So it is with us. As soon as we begin the process, we no longer need to wish today away hoping for a better tomorrow. We are no longer reactors to the situation but the creators of our own happily ever after.

CHAPTER 16

In Progress

Perfection does not exist. Still, we can chase it relentlessly, realizing that there is always room for improvement. As good as life gets, we can always make it better. If we dedicate ourselves to the long run and commit to running and living the edge each day, we will make consistent progress in the direction of our ideal selves.

We are runners. We have been to the other side of the mountain and seen the color blue. We know what it means to have initiative and integrity. We know how to be responsible, personable, adaptable, and determined. We understand how these attributes can make us more successful in running and in our other life stories. We have made a commitment to break free from the curse of normal and the chains of average as we work day after day, stride after stride, to close the gap between the runners and people we are, and the runners and people we want to be. We know there is no quick fix in this personal revolution, but through hard work and consistent effort, we can undergo personal transformation and create the lives we want to live. We understand that we all started out as children once upon a time and are working toward the best possible happily ever after. If we surround ourselves with kindred spirits who will join or support us in our journeys, we can get closer to the edge of our potentials than we ever could alone.

Writing this book has been a transformational experience for both of us. Just in putting these words and stories to paper, we have become more aware of who we are and who we can be. We have explored and deepened not only our own friendship, but also all the other important relationships in our lives.

Both of us believe that we are good people with happy and successful lives and life stories. At the same time, as we pointed out in Chapter 1, we have many imperfections. Gaining an understanding of these imperfections and how they affect our various life stories has allowed both of us to commit to addressing them so that we can direct our lives rather than simply react to the situation.

We are not done making mistakes and poor choices, but we have direction and purpose that make this journey so much more rewarding and enjoyable. We are distance mavens as long as we continue to work, strive, and improve ourselves in a relentless pursuit of excellence in everything.

Most importantly, we are sharing this journey with each other and now with you! Running the edge alone would not be half as much fun, so be sure to share this road with as many kindred spirits as you can find. Share your own stories, and look for the lessons learned as you laugh, cry, and inspire. Being a distance maven is not about who is the fastest runner, owns the biggest house, or has the largest bank account. It is about fulfilling the promise of your once upon a time by creating your happily ever after, one day and one stride at a time.

Early in this book, we encouraged you to commit to improving your running and life by following the way of the distance maven. At that moment, you turned a corner. You went from reacting to life to directing it. You no longer need to wait for a specific running pace, a position in a race, or even some situation in daily life to feel success-ful. With each stride you take, each morning you wake up full of ini-tiative and determination to put in the work, each risky attempt at something new, each moment of quiet contemplation about your life and your goals, you are running the edge. Like us, you are and always will be in progress. We are all distance mavens.

ACKNOWLEDGMENTS

We would like to thank the many people who supported us throughout the process of creating and writing this book. From the very beginning, when this book was just an idea without any substance, we had the unconditional support of our families and friends. Your belief in us and our ideas helped give us the confidence and motivation to begin. Thank you!

Thank you Alan Webb, Amy Yoder Begley, Chris Solinsky, Dathan Ritzenhein, Galen Rupp, Kara Goucher, and Paula Radcliffe for your help and contributions to this book.

To our chief council of high school runners who inspired us and gave us direction and support in the very beginning, we owe many thanks to Alli Billmeyer, Jack Driggs, Jeramy Elkaim, Elias Gedyon, Matt Jablonski, Rachel Johnson, Kelsey Margey, Catrina McAlister, Rebecca Mehra, Maddie Meyers, Ammar Moussa, Jim Rosa, Joe Rosa, Stephanie Schappert, Chelsey Sveinsson, Justin Vilhauer, and Zach Wills.

Special thanks to Scott Catalano, Phil Latter, Lois Ott, and April Thomas for being a some of the brave few to read and critique early drafts, Dave Holstrom for the help with graphic, website, and blog design, Todd Lile who helped shape many of the ideas and philosophies in this book.

To the "Run the Edge" community that follows us on facebook and on our blog, thank you for the positive energy and feedback! You embody what is right about the running community!

Tim

I would like to thank Jim and Robanette Catalano for being the best parents a runner could ever have and for supporting and believing in me in every crazy thing I have wanted to do in life including writing this book with Adam! Thanks to Ma Gouch also known as "Adam's mom" for the help editing, support, and free hugs. Thank you to my coaches, John Martin, Craig Luckasen, Mark Wetmore, and Jason Jensen as well as my teammates who helped me discover and develop a love of running. Thank you Amanda Felts; you didn't make the dedication page, but here you are in the acknowledgments! Thank you Northern Colorado Writers Group for helping me develop as a writer.

Finally a very special thanks to Adam Goucher who continues to inspire me to run and live the edge in everything I do! Thanks for never letting my dreams remain dreams. We did it my friend!

Adam

I would like to thank my incredible wife Kara for her unwavering support and belief in me even when I didn't believe in myself! To my son Colt, you are too young to read these words or understand how much you inspire me but I hope when you are old enough to read this book, you will be proud of your old man! Thank you to Judy Fellhauer, Mark Wetmore and Alberto Salazar for coaching me to being the best runner I could be and for helping mold me into the man I am today. A special thanks to my mom Lois Ott, and sisters, Cindy Edgar and Debbie Martinez for sticking by me in the best and worst of times and for all the love and support you continually give.

Finally a very special thanks to Tim Catalano for being the greatest friend anyone could ask for. You've challenged me to think outside the box and to be a better person and together we've accomplished things we'd only dreamt about! Here's to a life time of fun, challenging each other to run and live the edge!

ABOUT THE AUTHORS

TIM CATALANO

Tim, a highly recruited distance runner out of high school, went on to run varsity track and cross-country for the storied University of Colorado (CU) athletic program. While there, he helped the team earn fourth- and second-place finishes nationally. These experiences had a transformative influence on him that sparked a lifelong interest in the power of experience in shaping the individual.

He earned his undergraduate degree in psychology from CU in 1995 and added a master's degree in instruction and curriculum from the school's Department of Education in 1997. During his twelve-year teaching career, Tim worked at high schools in three countries. He taught IB psychology in the classroom and became heavily involved in high school athletics and activities outside the classroom. He was a head track and cross-country coach for ten years, created and sponsored two tremendously popular life improvement clubs for teens, and advised student governments for six years.

In 2007, Tim graduated from the Principals' Training Center with a certification in international school administration.

With a lifetime of involvement and interest in human behavior and the transformative influence of running and other activities, Tim has developed a passion to combine the teachings of psychology and the sport of running.

ADAM GOUCHER

Adam has a long list of accomplishments both as a student and as an athlete. In 1994, during his senior year of high school, he not only was the student body president but also managed to run away with the Foot Locker national cross-country championship. Adam signed with the University of Colorado as the nation's number one recruit and quickly made a name for himself by placing second at the NCAA cross-country championships in Arkansas and leading his team to a second-place finish. During his collegiate career, he was an eleven-time All American and captured four individual NCAA titles.

Before Adam graduated with a bachelor's degree in communications in 1998, he had already developed a passion for personal growth and began speaking with several local high schools about the value of running and setting goals.

After completing his collegiate career, Adam signed a contract with a shoe company to run professionally. He also continued to work with the CU men's and women's team as a volunteer assistant coach under Mark Wetmore. In his career, Adam has won eight individual U.S. championships and qualified for the finals in the world championships in track and cross country seven times. In 2000, Adam represented the United States in the Sydney Olympic Games.

Adam continues to run and battle through injury, but also has an eye toward giving back to a sport that has given him so much. He wishes to share his passion with other runners and use what he has learned from running to be not only the best athlete possible, but also the best husband, father, brother, son, and friend.